I0583328

# MAKING THE ARCHIVES TALK

THE PENN STATE SERIES IN THE HISTORY OF THE BOOK

*James L. W. West III, General Editor*

*Editorial Board*
Robert R. Edwards (Pennsylvania State University)
Paul Eggert (University of New South Wales at ADFA)
Simon Eliot (University of London)
William L. Joyce (Pennsylvania State University)
Beth Luey (Massachusetts Historical Society)
Jonathan Rose (Drew University)
Willa Z. Silverman (Pennsylvania State University)

Peter Burke, *The Fortunes of the "Courtier":*
*The European Reception of Castiglione's "Cortegiano"* (1996)

James M. Hutchisson, *The Rise of Sinclair Lewis, 1920–1930* (1996)

Julie Bates Dock, ed., *Charlotte Perkins Gilman's "The Yellow Wall-paper" and the*
*History of Its Publication and Reception: A Critical Edition and Documentary Casebook* (1998)

John Williams, ed., *Imaging the Early Medieval Bible* (1999)

Ezra Greenspan, *George Palmer Putnam: Representative American Publisher* (2000)

James G. Nelson, *Publisher to the Decadents: Leonard Smithers in the*
*Careers of Beardsley, Wilde, Dowson* (2000)

Pamela E. Selwyn, *Everyday Life in the German Book Trade: Friedrich Nicolai as*
*Bookseller and Publisher in the Age of Enlightenment* (2000)

David R. Johnson, *Conrad Richter: A Writer's Life* (2001)

David Finkelstein, *The House of Blackwood: Author-Publisher Relations*
*in the Victorian Era* (2002)

Rodger L. Tarr, ed., *As Ever Yours:*
*The Letters of Max Perkins and Elizabeth Lemmon* (2003)

Randy Robertson, *Censorship and Conflict in Seventeenth-Century England:*
*The Subtle Art of Division* (2009)

Catherine M. Parisian, ed., *The First White House Library:*
*A History and Annotated Catalogue* (2010)

Jane McLeod, *Licensing Loyalty: Printers, Patrons, and the State*
*in Early Modern France* (2011)

Charles Walton, ed., *Into Print: Limits and Legacies of the Enlightenment,*
*Essays in Honor of Robert Darnton* (2011)

# MAKING THE ARCHIVES TALK

*New and Selected Essays in Bibliography, Editing, and Book History*

James L. W. West III

The Pennsylvania State University Press
University Park, Pennsylvania

Library of Congress Cataloging-in-Publication Data

West, James L. W.
Making the archives talk : new and selected essays in
bibliography, editing, and book history /
James L. W. West, III.
p.    cm.—(The Penn State series
in the history of the book ; 16)
Includes bibliographical references and index.
Summary: "A collection of essays by editor, biographer,
bibliographer, and book historian James L. W. West III,
covering editorial theory, archival use, textual emendation,
and scholarly annotation. Discusses the treatment of both
public documents (novels, stories, nonfiction) and private
texts (letters, diaries, journals, working papers)"
—Provided by publisher.
ISBN 978-0-271-05067-6 (cloth : alk. paper)
ISBN 978-0-271-05068-3 (pbk. : alk. paper)
1. American literature—20th century—Criticism, Textual.
2. Editing.
3. Transmission of texts.
4. Dreiser, Theodore, 1871–1945.
5. Fitzgerald, F. Scott (Francis Scott), 1896–1940
6. Styron, William, 1925–2006.
I. Title.

PS80.W47 2011
808'.02—dc23
2011019812

Copyright © 2011 The Pennsylvania State University
All rights reserved
Printed in the United States of America
Published by The Pennsylvania State University Press,
University Park, PA 16802-1003

The Pennsylvania State University Press is a member of the
Association of American University Presses.

It is the policy of The Pennsylvania State University Press to
use acid-free paper. Publications on uncoated stock satisfy
the minimum requirements of American National Standard
for Information Sciences—Permanence of Paper for Printed
Library Material, ANSI Z39.48–1992.

*for my wife,*

MARY LEE CARNS

How can the world know anything so intimate as what we were intending to do? The answer is the world presumes to know.

—ROBERT FROST, "THE CONSTANT SYMBOL" (1946)

The thing that distinguishes cultural work from other types of work is that it's never over. It keeps evolving, it keeps developing; it's not a business plan, but it's constantly evolving something from the past to the future. And the most important thing about the work is that you don't give up.

—YO-YO MA, *VIRTUOSO VOICES*, NATIONAL PUBLIC RADIO, 12 OCTOBER 2009

You'd sniffled through an era's must,
Filling your nostrils up with dust,
And then, arising from your knees,
Published, in one gigantic sneeze . . .

—F. SCOTT FITZGERALD, *THIS SIDE OF PARADISE* (1920)

# CONTENTS

~

LIST OF ILLUSTRATIONS / *ix*

Introduction / *1*

The Scholarly Editor as Biographer / *6*

Editorial Theory and the Act of Submission / *17*

Fair Copy, Authorial Intention, and Versioning / *29*

Alcohol and Drinking in *Sister Carrie* / *39*

Double Quotes and Double Meanings in *Jennie Gerhardt* / *47*

Editing Private Papers: Three Examples from Dreiser / *60*

Toxic Words and the Editor / *73*

Did F. Scott Fitzgerald Have the Right Publisher? / *88*

The Internal Chronology of *Tender Is the Night* / *102*

Annotating Mr. Fitzgerald / *115*

Keeper of the Flame:
Editing the Literary Remains of William Styron / *125*

The End Is Near / *135*

ACKNOWLEDGMENTS / *145*

INDEX / *147*

# ILLUSTRATIONS

∼

1   Leaf 516 from the working typescript of
William Styron's *Lie Down in Darkness* (1951)   /   *13*

2   Page 422 from the 1911 Harper first edition of *Jennie Gerhardt*   /   *49*

3   Leaf 164 of Theodore Dreiser's Russian diary   /   *67*

4   Leaf 31 from the working typescript of
F. Scott Fitzgerald's "A Snobbish Story"   /   *84*

5   Copyright page of the twelfth trade impression of
*This Side of Paradise* (1920)   /   *92*

6   Leaf 1, holograph of Styron's statement on
the Bill Clinton–Monica Lewinsky scandal   /   *132*

# INTRODUCTION

Good editors are good narrators. In constructing their editions they tell two stories. The primary narrative gives an account of how the literary work came into being; the secondary narrative tells how the editor gathered the evidence, evaluated it, and established the text. Both narratives are essential to the success of the edition.

The primary narrative tells how the work was conceived, composed, revised, and polished; how it was submitted to publishers, accepted for print, and put into production; how it moved through the publication process, with further revision and refinement and sometimes with cutting and bowdlerization; and how it was released as a published artifact. Many of these primary narratives are stories about overcoming obstacles to arrive at goals, achievements, victories. The best narratives include drama and suspense. The author—whether young and apprehensive, middle-aged and experienced, or old and weary—can face an array of challenges. These typically include lack of money, poor health, doubts about the material, difficulties in love, flagging confidence, and personal demons such as alcoholism and mental illness. The challenges are met: the result is a literary work of merit, created for an audience which the author can only imagine during the act of composition. This audience materializes soon or late and gives way to other audiences of readers, teachers, and critics who hold the work in high esteem. The author persevered during the original period of creation. The work was finished and published; it ascended into the canon; decades later it is still read and studied. A scholarly edition of this work is now needed.

In order to write such a narrative, an editor must "make the archives talk"—hence the title of this collection. The editor must examine the surviving notes, manuscripts, typescripts, proofs, and other evidence. The editor must also read the relevant letters and journals and study the publishers' records and account books. From these materials an account of the composition of the work can be fashioned. The narrative will be assembled from evidence that is otherwise inert. One does not "allow" the archives to talk; one "makes" them talk, crafting stories in the same way that biographers and historians do, by selecting and arranging the evidence and writing a story that ties the whole together.

The secondary narrative is equally important. It follows naturally from the primary narrative, running beneath and parallel to it. The secondary narrative is often a "quest" story—the editor's account of gathering and evaluating materials, searching for error or interference, and presenting the text in a new form. The editor has devoted much time to the task, locating documents and fugitive materials and comparing incarnations of the work to one another in order to arrive at a different text—this in service of the author, the reader, and literature. This secondary narrative (though not written with the pronoun *I*) is presented in the editor's voice.

Both narratives are fabrications, constructed from documents and other testimony at hand, often fragmentary or incomplete, and including both facts and imagined reconstructions. Editorial narratives are shaped by selection, emphasis, and vocabulary. They can confirm the soundness of the received text or call for a different text. Frequently the evidence can be made to support either argument.

Several of the essays in this volume are narratives of this kind, intended to validate an editorial approach to a particular text. The first three essays are abstract and theoretical; most of the others involve the editing and annotation of specific texts. I have drawn on some forty years of experience for my examples. The authors whose works I have edited during my career are Theodore Dreiser, F. Scott Fitzgerald, and William Styron—all twentieth-century American writers best known for their novels, short stories, and nonfiction. The problems found in their texts and the availability of extensive collections of their papers have shaped my view of scholarly editing. These are not obscure authors: their writings have been widely read and praised. Their books sold well during their careers and continue to sell today—a fact of which I have been conscious while editing. Dreiser, Fitzgerald, and Styron have thousands of contemporary readers, not only in the academy but also among the laity. I have wanted to produce editions that would appeal to these readers and be useful to them.

I am an intentionalist editor. I believe that authors have intentions for their writings, that these intentions change over time, and that particular sets of intentions can be recaptured, though never fully or perfectly. The best method of recapture is eclectic emendation, which brings together readings from several witnesses or versions (when they survive) to form a new text. This text will be as close to the desired ideal as scholarly labor and imaginative reconstruction can bring it.

Classic Greg-Bowers copy-text procedures, usually associated with intentionalist editing, are not well suited to the editing of twentieth-century works, especially if manuscripts, typescripts, and proofs are extant. But intentionalist editing and the creation of eclectic texts, with readings drawn from more than one witness, can be executed without copy-text procedures. Editing without a copy-text, in fact, frees the editor from the tyranny of such a document and makes it easier to regard the text as fluid and unsettled.[1] One eclectic text can be created and published from among many that are possible. Other editors, interpreting the same evidence in different ways, can create and publish their own texts, once the work has passed into the public domain.

The editorial theorists who have most strongly influenced my practice, without necessarily agreeing with all of my views, are G. Thomas Tanselle, Peter Shillingsburg, George Bornstein, and Paul Eggert. Tanselle's insights about authorial intention and copy-text editing have been illuminating; Shillingsburg's flexibility and openness to new thinking have been exemplary; Bornstein's emphasis on the original sites of publication has been educative; Eggert's restoration of authorial agency and his inclusion of the editor, from the beginning, in the history of the text have been liberating.[2]

I have not been persuaded by the writings of editorial theorists who want to see all texts as socially constructed and therefore inviolable.[3] Texts are certainly shaped by the circumstances of their making and publication, but it does not follow that they cannot be significantly emended with readings from other witnesses, unless the purpose of literary interpretation is to duplicate the reactions of original readers to original texts—an impossible task. Most of these theorists eschew eclectic editing; they use instead an approach that is sometimes called "versioning."[4] In its essentials, this is historical or documentary editing, with the editor's role largely confined to transcribing, annotating, and (in a limited way) interpreting. The role of the author is diminished and sometimes subordinated to the activities of spouses, friends, amanuenses, typists, publishers, copyeditors, book designers, typesetters, and proofreaders. The moral stance of the editor—his or her sense of putting things to rights—is likewise diminished.

The labor required to produce a versionist or historical edition is almost the same as that needed for an eclectic edition, but the text presented is a preexisting one, lightly emended or not emended at all. To me this avoids the responsibility and great pleasure of scholarly editing—to repair an old text or put into play a new one. This new text will itself have been socially constructed, as will the two editorial narratives. The process of social construction for the new text will have been superior to, or certainly different from, the process that produced the old text. The new text will need interpretation. The process will continue; it cannot be arrested or frozen in time.

Versionist or historical editors are often hobbled by theory and paralyzed by overanalysis. Their procedures undercut both the primary and secondary editorial narratives. The author becomes only one among many actors; the editor becomes primarily a copyist and annotator. Almost the only possible errors that an editor of this persuasion can make are those of transcription or reproduction. Little is attempted: the evidence is presented neutrally to an imagined audience of readers and critics who are invited to evaluate and react to it. This audience, however, seems rarely to emerge. One does not often see ponderings on variant passages in the pages of scholarly journals or hear debates about the superiority of this reading over that reading at academic conferences. Most rank-and-file critics and teachers of literature have not been trained to use scholarly editions and are not especially interested in learning how to do so. Versionist editing validates the inertia of this group. Misoneism, or resistance to change, is endemic among humanists and dovetails with versionist editing. Scholarly editors are left open to a familiar charge—that what they do does not matter and is little more than sophisticated secretarial work.

Social constructionists have had the good effect of ridding the field of much hubris and overstatement. It is no longer acceptable to refer to a text as "definitive" or, except in the simplest of cases, to claim that a text will never need to be edited again. Versioning and historical editing function well for short works of poetry and for stories and essays that survive in unique texts or discrete versions. (In such cases, of course, there is little question about how the texts will be edited.) I have used versionist techniques, most notably on Fitzgerald's short novel *Trimalchio,* the penultimate version of *The Great Gatsby.* For most of the texts I have edited, however, I have sought to recapture authorial intentions by using eclectic techniques. For me historical or versionist editing is overly mechanical and defensive, placing too great a value on consistency. Intentionalist editing, by contrast, takes an offensive stance. It is a human enterprise, therefore imperfect and inevitably inconsistent.

The age of digital texts has arrived and promises much to scholarly editors. It is possible already to present multiple texts, corrected or not, emended or not, blended or not, using eclectic techniques or historical methods or both simultaneously. The next generation of scholarly editors will work (perhaps altogether) in a digital environment. But if digital editions become nothing more than collection points at which to store archival evidence in the hope that someone will use it, then we will not have advanced. I have worked always in paper and ink; I seek the permanence of a printed text. With a text fixed in print, an editor can be wrong. An editor can also be right. Editors, in my view, should interpret evidence, fashion narratives, make decisions, and take chances. They should see their decisions into print and accept responsibility for them.

Competition among editorial approaches will continue. The shuttlecock, in Dr. Johnson's formulation, will be struck on both sides of the net and thus be kept aloft. Disagreements will persist; new editions will appear. Two hundred years from now a young editor will use my work on Fitzgerald as the basis for the first old-spelling edition of *The Great Gatsby*. Editing abides. I take comfort in that.

NOTES

1. See G. Thomas Tanselle, "Editing Without a Copy-Text," *Studies in Bibliography* 47 (1994): 1–22.

2. G. Thomas Tanselle, *Literature and Artifacts* (Charlottesville: Bibliographical Society of the University of Virginia, 1998); Tanselle, *Textual Criticism and Scholarly Editing* (Charlottesville: University Press of Virginia, 1990); Tanselle, *A Rationale of Textual Criticism* (Philadelphia: University of Pennsylvania Press, 1989); Peter L. Shillingsburg, *Scholarly Editing in the Computer Age: Theory and Practice*, 3rd ed. (Ann Arbor: University of Michigan Press, 1996); Shillingsburg, *Resisting Texts: Authority and Submission in Constructions of Meaning* (Ann Arbor: University of Michigan Press, 1997); Shillingsburg, *From Gutenberg to Google: Electronic Representations of Literary Texts* (Cambridge: Cambridge University Press, 2006); George Bornstein, *Material Modernism: The Politics of the Page* (Cambridge: Cambridge University Press, 2001); Paul Eggert, *Securing the Past: Conservation in Art, Architecture, and Literature* (Cambridge: Cambridge University Press, 2009).

3. I have in mind here James Thorpe, *Principles of Textual Criticism* (San Marino, Calif.: Huntington Library, 1972), esp. chaps. 1–3; Morse Peckham, "Reflections on the Foundations of Modern Textual Editing," *Proof* 1 (1971): 122–55; Philip Gaskell, *A New Introduction to Bibliography* (New York: Oxford University Press, 1972), esp. "Textual Bibliography," 336–60; Gaskell, *From Writer to Reader: Studies in Editorial Method* (Oxford: Clarendon Press, 1978); Jerome J. McGann, *A Critique of Modern Textual Criticism* (Chicago: University of Chicago Press, 1983); McGann, *The Textual Condition* (Princeton: Princeton University Press, 1991); D. F. McKenzie, *Bibliography and the Sociology of Texts* (London: British Library, 1986).

4. Best described by Donald Reiman in the chapter "'Versioning': The Presentation of Multiple Texts," in *Romantic Texts and Contexts* (Columbia: University of Missouri Press, 1987), 167–80.

# THE SCHOLARLY EDITOR AS BIOGRAPHER

Of the subdisciplines practiced in and around departments of English, scholarly editing looks to be one of the few with an empirical foundation. Editors gather and analyze physical evidence; they present it in the form of facsimiles, variant tables, stemmas, and lists of emendations. Much of the theoretical writing published by editors has an empirical cast, often concerning itself with the rules by which evidence should be interpreted. We appear to be empiricists to those outside the humanities, a perception that many of us welcome. It is almost uniformly believed by those who control the budgets of American universities that truth can best be apprehended through empirical methods and the collection of data. Thus scholarly editors are at an advantage: they can explain to their deans how they marshal and deploy evidence and why their work has utilitarian importance.

In this essay, however, I want to suggest that scholarly editing is not at base an empirical pursuit. It has empirical features, but fundamentally it relies on intuition and imagination more heavily than it does on analysis of evidence. At its very center scholarly editing is a species of *biography,* one of the most slippery and difficult-to-define varieties of writing. As editors analyze their variants, they are practicing biography. They are constructing in their minds a conception of the author's creative personality that will undergird all that they, as editors, wish to do with the texts.

Scholarly editing, like biography, is a human activity, flawed and subject to emotion and error. Like biography, editing is an attempt to capture and describe moments of behavior from the past. Biography and editing employ many of the same techniques and much of the same material; both can be hobbled by too little or too much information. The biographer and the editor ask essentially the same questions: Why did my subject behave in this way? Did he really do what he appears to have done, or is the evidence incomplete or misleading? Did her decisions spring naturally from her desires and prejudices, or was she under heavy influence from others? Was she prevented from taking action or speaking out by social or legal constraints? Did he want matters to turn out as they did, or did he acquiesce from inertia or weariness or a sense of helplessness?

Biographers ask these questions about a great range of behaviors involving childhood, upbringing, education, marriage, finances, sexual preference, political allegiance, and public success. Scholarly editors focus more selectively on the composition and publication of literary works, but their investigations still concern these same matters. Editors must have in their minds fully fleshed-out portraits of their authors as they attempt to reconstruct what those authors did, or how they felt about the works that were passing into print.

Ideally editors begin by examining the evidence dispassionately and developing conclusions about authors' composing methods and their attitudes toward collaboration or interference from others. Few editors, however, begin with a blank slate. Most of them already have preconceptions about their authors, notions taken from biographers, critics, and other editors who have come before. Such notions cause editors to view the evidence from the beginning in a slanted way. Perhaps editors want to strike out in new directions, reassessing their authors' views on writing and the publishing industry. In these cases editors act as revisionist biographers, arguing (from new facts, if available) that their authors were not the people previous editors thought them to be.

Most editors decide ahead of time how they wish to edit a given text. They know which text (of the several that can be constructed from the evidence) they want to publish. Perhaps this text will be essentially the one that has been in circulation all along, with a few adjustments and corrections; perhaps it will be a radically different text that must be resurrected from early drafts or proofs. In either case the editor begins biographically, by constructing an author who will approve (posthumously) of the text that is going to be published. One is reminded of the Queen at the Knave's trial in chapter 12 of *Alice's Adventures in Wonderland:* "No, no!" cries the Queen. "Sentence first—verdict afterwards."

Much of the discussion about theories of scholarly editing is actually about biography. Editors are not talking about technique or logic; they are instead considering authors' personalities and the decisions they imagine these authors to have made at particular moments in the past. Toward that end editors have developed certain precut patterns that they use to describe their authors. An editor usually selects one of these patterns and then proceeds to edit, basing assumptions about past behavior on the pattern. One might, for example, choose to depict an author as young and innocent, ignorant of the ways of the publishing industry, powerless in dealing with its bureaucracy, and anxious to make concessions in order to see a work appear between hard covers. This authorial personality would require an editing style valuing early intention over later compromise. Alternately, one might portray this same young novelist as talented but callow, inclined to produce overwrought and sophomoric writing, grateful (especially in retrospect) for the guiding hand of the older, wiser trade editor, pleased that her excesses were curbed or his writing toned down for public consumption. Such an authorial personality would justify an editing strategy designed to validate the received text. Both of these approaches could be applied to the same author and work. It is all a matter of language, of choosing a particular set of verbs, adjectives, and adverbs that will construct, as a biographer would, the author necessary to justify the editorial approach.

When this constructed author matches the standard biographical portrait, the edited text is usually received with approval, but when the portrait differs from the accepted picture, one often encounters resistance. Some examples from the texts of Theodore Dreiser will help to clarify this point. Many early biographers and critics viewed Dreiser as uneducated and crude, both as an artist and a man. He was seen as a writer who could produce prose on demand but who needed help with spelling, grammar, style, and content. Dreiser was portrayed as a child who resisted (but still required) chastisement with the blue pencil. The trade editors and quasi-collaborators who worked on his writings were seen as morally superior to him. If he did not approve of what they did to his texts (and often he did not), then he *should* have approved of it. A particular array of adjectives and adverbs helped to create this portrait. Dreiser was "careless," "inattentive," and "slap-dash"; he worked "rapidly" and "hastily"; he was "disinclined" to do the difficult labor of revision and was "indifferent" about the accuracy and grammatical correctness of his writings. His style was "clumsy" and "opaque." Revisions made by editors and amanuenses to improve the readability of his prose, or to excise crudities of thought or expression from it, should be judged favorably. Dreiser's work was believed to require a documentary or historical approach. The received text, no matter how much altered by the people through whose hands it had passed, should be validated. Selected passages from early drafts might be included in notes and appendixes as scraps from the worktable, or as examples of the gracelessness of Dreiser's unedited prose, but the text that should be read and critiqued was the one that was already in print.

This view, however, did not always match the extant evidence, as many biographical portraits do not. Certainly there was data to support a view of Dreiser as unlettered, feckless, and boorish; but there was equally good evidence on which to base a different picture. Dreiser could be seen, alternately, as unsystematically but broadly read, unpolished and blunt but egalitarian and honest, and (most importantly) as disciplined and methodical in his writing habits. Evidence to support both views survives, sometimes in irritating profusion. Dreiser's manuscripts and correspondence show that he was sometimes attentive and sometimes careless about his texts, alternately painstaking and casual about their revision, and both prickly about their alteration by others and indifferent to their fate once they left his desk. Dreiser's own conception of literary composition swung between two poles. Sometimes he saw it as a community enterprise involving himself, his wife, his lovers of the moment, and various friends and advisors. At other times he saw himself as a solitary, prophet-like seer who was in contact with the muses and whose utterances should not be meddled with.

When I set out to re-edit *Sister Carrie* (1900), Dreiser's famous first novel, and *Jennie Gerhardt* (1911), his undervalued second novel, I had available the makings of almost any biographical portrait I wished to present.[1] What I needed was a Dreiser who would justify the approach I meant to take, an approach that would put into print earlier and very different texts from the ones that had been available. I believed that these new texts would represent Dreiser's intentions more faithfully than the published texts did. In the introductions and other ancillary matter for the editions of *Sister Carrie* and *Jennie Gerhardt*, I therefore presented the Dreiser I needed—an author more attentive to his texts and more troubled about editorial tampering than earlier critics and editors had admitted. I used an alternate vocabulary for describing him at work. He was not "plodding" but rather "steady." His style was "blunt" and "unadorned" instead of "clumsy" and "inept." He was "intellectually restless" and had a "wide-ranging curiosity," not a "wandering attention span" and an "unfocused intelligence." He wrote "fluently" and worked with great "self-discipline" and "doggedness," yielding authority over his texts only when faced with rigid deadlines and obdurate publishing houses. Having established this conception of Dreiser and his intentions, I could analyze the evidence and construct the texts I wanted. My problem was to create a Dreiser who cared enough about his textual virtue for me to defend it.

The issue is not whether the new texts of *Sister Carrie* or *Jennie Gerhardt* that I published were superior to the old ones, more faithful to real life or more complex or moving. Such evaluations are individual and personal: for me the new texts were better than the old ones, but that is all that I (or any editor) can say. Nor is the issue whether my revised biographical portrait of Dreiser was more nearly valid than earlier portraits. I believe that it was, but biography is so nebulous a discipline that these judgments cannot be made reliably. The important thing in this example is, rather, the sequence in which the thinking took place. Were the texts based on preexisting biographical portraits of Dreiser, or was a revised portrait developed to validate the radically different texts? I am certain that the second sequence took place. I knew ahead of time which texts of *Sister Carrie* and *Jennie Gerhardt* I wanted to present. I worked as a biographer to create an author who also wanted these texts to come to life.

It was relatively easy to proceed in this fashion because a great amount was known about Dreiser's life. By the mid-1970s, when I began work on *Sister Carrie,* he had been the subject of two major biographies, and many of his friends and associates had published reminiscences of him. Dreiser was a newsworthy figure for much of his life; one therefore had reportage, interviews, profiles, and book reviews to draw upon. He was a pack rat who saved virtually everything: manuscripts, proofs, diaries, letters, maps, ticket stubs, menus, photographs—nearly all of it preserved in his papers at the University of Pennsylvania or in collections at other libraries. All of this was useful material for a biographer-*cum*-editor.

What would happen, though, if a scholarly editor had to investigate a figure about whom much less was known and for whom a much smaller body of evidence was extant? Such situations have arisen fairly frequently with twentieth-century texts that resulted from collaborations between authors and trade editors. Editors at trade houses were often immensely influential on particular literary works, but little has been known about most of them— about their rearing and education, prejudices and blind spots, tastes and preferences and standards. Sometimes the scholarly editor has been lucky: Maxwell Perkins, the famous figure at Charles Scribner's Sons who handled the writings of F. Scott Fitzgerald, Ernest Hemingway, and Thomas Wolfe, left behind hundreds of letters in the Scribner files (housed at Princeton University Library) and was the subject of a two-part *New Yorker* profile in 1944 and a full-length biography in 1978.[2] Other editors have not been so thoroughly investigated. Saxe Commins, who edited William Faulkner, Gertrude Stein, Eugene O'Neill, William Saroyan, and Robinson Jeffers at Random House, is an obscure figure. A substantial amount of material by and about him survives in the Random House papers at Columbia University, and his widow published a volume of laudatory writing about him in 1978, but his personality remains something of a mystery.[3] Ripley Hitchcock, who edited Stephen Crane at Appleton and Dreiser at Harper and Brothers, is more obscure still, although a small collection of his papers survives at the Butler Library, Columbia University. And almost nothing is known about Tom Smith, who oversaw the cutting and shaping of Dreiser's *An American Tragedy* at Liveright in 1924. Many of the Liveright records were lost when the firm went belly-up in 1932; a few items survive, but they tell us little about Smith.

Knowledge of such spear-carriers as Perkins, Commins, Hitchcock, and Smith is often of crucial importance to the scholarly editor. What role did Perkins play in the composition of certain of Hemingway's books—*Death in the Afternoon*, for example? What combination of personal politics and company rules prompted Commins to cut ten poems from Jeffers's *The Double Axe* in 1947? What conception of woman's place in society caused Hitchcock to oversee an editing job on Dreiser's *Jennie Gerhardt* that diminished the role of the title character? What mixture of literary judgment and marketplace economics guided Smith as he shepherded *An American Tragedy* into print?

In the absence of biographical data, scholarly editors who address these questions have usually applied precut biographical patterns to trade editors, just as they have to authors. The trade editor has been depicted as a bland representative of the publishing establishment and, by extension, as a conservative, limiting, cautionary force. Then, according to the scholarly editor's inclinations for the text, the author has either been allowed to rebel against this avuncular figure or has been made to knuckle under to him. Proceeding in this way is simplistic: anyone who has studied carefully the blue-pencilings of a given editor on a particular manuscript or set of proofs can testify that many of the suggestions, revisions, and bowdlerizations seem more personal and idiosyncratic than they do representative of company policy or of the standards of the dominant culture. One has little choice, however, if the materials are scanty. One is forced to function as would a biographer who possesses little evidence, which is to say that one is thrown back on imagination and speculation.

At least the scholarly editor can imagine and speculate with impunity because all of these authors, trade editors, lovers, advisors, and amanuenses are safely in the great beyond. Dreiser, for example, died in 1945; he cannot object if a biographer's or editor's portrait of him seems skewed. No one thought to ask Dreiser in detail before he died about his attitudes toward the editing of his texts. Indeed no one knew (other than anecdotally) how extensively they had been cut, revised, and bowdlerized until well after his death, when his manuscripts and other papers came to the University of Pennsylvania and began to be studied. Thus in the absence of specific instructions from Dreiser, editor/biographers have been free to follow their own instincts.[4]

But what if a living author *is* asked such questions about his or her texts? By way of illustration I shall offer a story about William Styron, whose manuscripts and texts I have studied and whose biography I have written.[5] Styron's mature fiction was bleached and banned from time to time in various countries, most notably in the United Kingdom, but the incident that brings issues of scholarly editing most clearly to light comes from early in his career. It involves the prepublication cutting and revision of his first novel, *Lie Down in Darkness,* issued in 1951 by Bobbs-Merrill.

Styron submitted his manuscript to Bobbs-Merrill in the spring of 1951. The decision was overwhelmingly for acceptance, but with the stipulation that Styron would have to tone down some of the language in Peyton Loftis's interior monologue, a long Molly Bloom–like section near the end of the narrative that occurs just before she takes her own life. At issue were references to genitalia, menstruation, and promiscuous sex, plus some hints about a possibly incestuous relationship with her father. Hiram Haydn, Styron's editor at Bobbs-Merrill, brokered the changes, soothing Styron's ruffled feelings and arguing that the novel was too good to risk its being misapprehended as a "dirty" book, rather as J. D. Salinger's *The Catcher in the Rye* (also published in 1951) would become, or as *Ulysses* had often been viewed in the decade just after its publication in 1922. Styron yielded to this logic and permitted two rounds of cuts.[6]

I had assumed that if the chance ever presented itself for a restoration of this material, Styron would take it. I had instinctively adopted a precut pattern in constructing a portrait of him as young and powerless, willing to let his first novel be compromised if it would get him into print and mentioned on the book review pages of major magazines and newspapers. But I was wrong. In 1991 Random House, Styron's publisher since 1956, acquired the copyright for *Lie Down in Darkness* from Bobbs-Merrill and announced plans to publish the text in a uniform edition. I asked Styron if he would like to have the censored passages restored to Peyton's soliloquy, and he said that he would. But once I had disinterred the words and phrases from his manuscripts at the Library of Congress, he changed his mind. The cuts and revisions recommended by Hiram Haydn, he now said, struck him as judicious and proper. The text should stand as originally published. Thus the Random House reissue of *Lie Down in Darkness* appeared in 1992 without significant change (a few

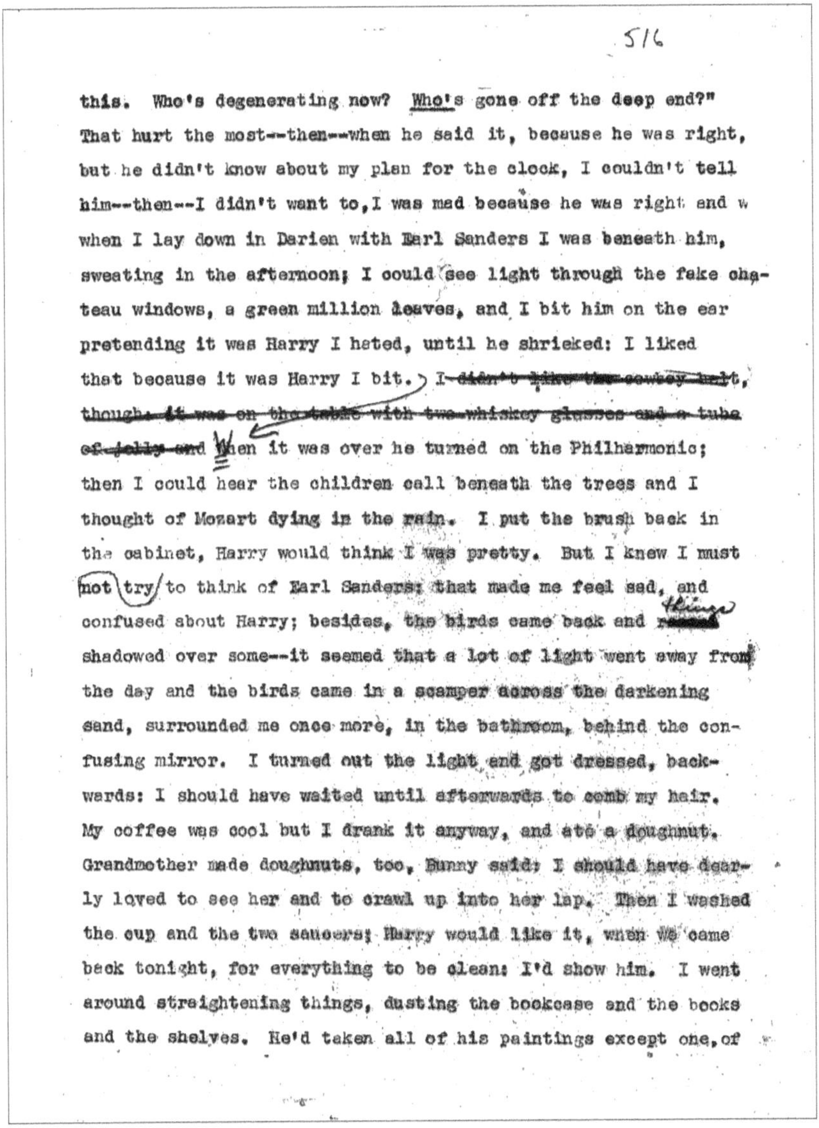

516

this. Who's degenerating now? Who's gone off the deep end?"
That hurt the most--then--when he said it, because he was right,
but he didn't know about my plan for the clock, I couldn't tell
him--then--I didn't want to, I was mad because he was right and w
when I lay down in Darien with Earl Sanders I was beneath him,
sweating in the afternoon; I could see light through the fake cha-
teau windows, a green million leaves, and I bit him on the ear
pretending it was Harry I hated, until he shrieked: I liked
that because it was Harry I bit. ~~I didn't like the cowboy belt,
though, it was on the table with two whiskey glasses and a tube
of jelly and~~ When it was over he turned on the Philharmonic;
then I could hear the children call beneath the trees and I
thought of Mozart dying in the rain. I put the brush back in
the cabinet, Harry would think I was pretty. But I knew I must
not try to think of Earl Sanders; that made me feel sad, and
confused about Harry; besides, the birds came back and ~~returned~~ things
shadowed over some--it seemed that a lot of light went away from
the day and the birds came in a scamper across the darkening
sand, surrounded me once more, in the bathroom, behind the confusing mirror. I turned out the light and got dressed, back-
wards: I should have waited until afterwards to comb my hair.
My coffee was cool but I drank it anyway, and ate a doughnut.
Grandmother made doughnuts, too, Bunny said: I should have dearly loved to see her and to crawl up into her lap. Then I washed
the cup and the two saucers; Harry would like it, when we came
back tonight, for everything to be clean: I'd show him. I went
around straightening things, dusting the bookcase and the books
and the shelves. He'd taken all of his paintings except one, of

*Fig. 1* Leaf 516 from the working typescript of William Styron's *Lie Down in Darkness* (1951). Styron was under pressure from his publisher, Bobbs-Merrill, to dial down the sexual temperature of this section. On this leaf he has altered references to a "cowboy belt" and a "tube of jelly." William Styron Papers, Manuscript Division, Library of Congress.

typos were corrected), and the received text was validated.[7] My own disappointment was tempered by the fact that I agreed with Styron. The unsavory details, reinserted into Peyton's deranged monologue, would have transformed her into a less sympathetic figure than she had been in the Bobbs-Merrill text. One would not have pitied her or identified so closely with her.

Many influences were operating here. Styron was making his decisions as a mature writer in his sixties; he had not recovered fully from a period of severe depression and was apprehensive about his literary reputation. Perhaps it was best not to rock the boat. Haydn had been a friend and mentor to him. It might have seemed ungrateful to disavow his work on the text of *Lie Down in Darkness* these many years later. Probably Styron could no longer remember exactly how he felt in 1951 when Bobbs-Merrill required him to bowdlerize his text. His intentions in 1991 had little to do with his intentions in 1951, and in any case the earlier intentions could only be divined tangentially from Hiram Haydn's letters *to* him because Haydn had not saved Styron's side of the correspondence. My own reaction, though finally unimportant, was influenced by Styron's. The authority in this case was his; perhaps that is why I felt immediately that he was right.

In 1995, three years after the unrestored *Lie Down in Darkness* had been reprinted in the Vintage uniform edition, I again asked Styron about the bowdlerized passages. Did he think that it might be appropriate someday to publish a restored text in a different form—a facsimile of the original holograph, perhaps, or an edition published by a university press? This time he said yes, so long as the restored text did not replace the text published in 1951. That text should not be withdrawn from the market. I made a mental note of his response, thinking that in a year or two I might propose an edition of Peyton's monologue to a university press or perhaps to a publisher of limited signed editions. I would secure formal approval for the project from Styron at that point and, equally important, would seek the blessing of Random House. Other projects intervened, however, and the moment to make such a proposal never arrived.

Styron died in November 2006. Control of his literary estate passed to his widow, Rose, and to his children. The Library of America, a publisher that has issued restored editions of other American authors (Richard Wright and Raymond Carver, for example), is interested in publishing two volumes of Styron's writings. The Library of America might be an appropriate place to publish the unexpurgated text, with the proviso that the 1951 text would still be available from Random House. This approach would make available

Styron's original text for Peyton's monologue, the text as he composed it rather than as he revised it under pressure from Bobbs-Merrill. Critics should enjoy chewing over the differences. The Styron heirs would have to decide whether to go ahead with this plan. Fortunately all versions of the text survive in Styron's papers at the Library of Congress. The unexpurgated text, it seems to me, ought eventually to be published.

This question is in remission for now, but texts remain unstable and liable to change. How will an editor many years from now view the situation, once *Lie Down in Darkness* enters the public domain and can be reedited by anyone? The answer is that such an editor will be able to view it in almost any way that he or she chooses. Evidence survives to depict Styron, in 1951, as angry and frustrated with the timidity of Bobbs-Merrill. Evidence of equal weight exists to portray him as grateful for Haydn's guidance and judiciousness. The issue for our hypothetical future editor might come down to his or her interpretation of Peyton's character, as it is revealed in the monologue. Which Peyton will our future editor prefer? The sexually adventurous Peyton of the manuscripts and typescripts, or the more ethereal and abstracted Peyton of the published book? Just as important, which William Styron (presented biographically) will approve of the Peyton that the editor chooses? How will that Styron be created? How will his imprimatur be placed on the text?

The technology will surely exist by then to allow our editor some flexibility. If we are viewing most texts on screens, and if those texts are sufficiently fluid, then Styron's readers should be able to experience the two texts alternately, or superimposed one on the other, or side by side in double columns. We have the technology to make this happen now. Who knows what we will be capable of in the years to come?

One thing is certain, though: editors in that future time will still be proceeding biographically as much as they will be operating empirically. Before they take action to validate a received text or present a new one, they will have to establish in their minds some reasonably firm conclusions about their authors' personalities and preferences. They will find themselves working in reverse order, deciding first what texts they want to bring to life and then creating authors who will approve of what they want to do.

NOTES

1. The two texts in question are from the University of Pennsylvania Dreiser edition: Theodore Dreiser, *Sister Carrie,* historical eds., John C. Berkey and Alice M. Winters; textual ed., James L. W. West III; gen. ed., Neda M. Westlake (Philadelphia: University of Pennsylvania Press, 1981); and Dreiser,

*Jennie Gerhardt,* ed. James L. W. West III (Philadelphia: University of Pennsylvania Press, 1992). Page numbers from these two editions will be cited parenthetically in later essays in this collection.

2. Malcolm Cowley, "Unshaken Friend," *New Yorker,* 1 and 8 April 1944; A. Scott Berg, *Max Perkins: Editor of Genius* (New York: E. P. Dutton, 1978).

3. Dorothy Commins, *What Is an Editor? Saxe Commins at Work* (Chicago: University of Chicago Press, 1978); see also *"Love and Admiration and Respect": The O'Neill-Commins Correspondence,* ed. Dorothy Commins (Durham: Duke University Press, 1986).

4. In letters to H. L. Mencken, Dreiser did imply that he hoped his autobiographical volume *Dawn* might one day be published in uncut form. See, for example, Dreiser to Mencken, 24 June 1916, in *Dreiser-Mencken Letters: The Correspondence of Theodore Dreiser and H. L. Mencken, 1907–1945,* ed. Thomas P. Riggio, 2 vols. (Philadelphia: University of Pennsylvania Press, 1986), 1:239.

5. James L. W. West III, *William Styron: A Life* (New York: Random House, 1998).

6. See Arthur D. Casciato, "His Editor's Hand: Hiram Haydn's Changes in *Lie Down in Darkness,*" in *Critical Essays on William Styron,* ed. Arthur D. Casciato and James L. W. West III (Boston: G. K. Hall, 1982), 36–46.

7. This text was published in the Vintage uniform edition of Styron's writings. The *Lie Down in Darkness* volume appeared in January 1992.

# EDITORIAL THEORY AND THE ACT OF SUBMISSION

For the scholarly editor, a crucial moment in the compositional history of a literary work is the point at which the author submits the work to a publisher. In a literal sense this moment occurs when the author (or a representative) places a copy of the text, usually a manuscript or typescript, into the publisher's hands. This act has symbolic significance: the author is releasing control over the text and watching it enter the publication process, a sequence of operations that will transform it from a private document, existing in a single copy, to a public document, existing in multiple copies.

The word *submit* sums up much of the symbolism of the act. Authors are submitting their work to a process that is likely to require compromises. Experienced writers know that they must be prepared to defend their work. They know that they will probably have to give in to some of the publisher's suggestions, or, less pleasantly, to submit to the publisher's demands. Authors also know that there are parts of the publication process over which they will have little control; on these matters they will have no choice but to submit. They must trust their publishers to act in a fiduciary way, much as a physician acts on behalf of a patient or an attorney in the interests of a client.

Scholarly editors invest the act of submission with much symbolic significance. According to one's persuasion, the act of submission can be viewed in terms that are positive, negative, or mixed. For some editors the moment, viewed retrospectively, is an unhappy one. These editors expect to discover that the publisher has performed operations upon the text, that most of these operations have been harmful, and that the text has emerged at publication time in a scarred and battered state. For these editors, the moment of submission might be likened to watching a suitcase being placed on a conveyor belt behind the counter of a budget airline.

To another group of scholarly editors, the moment of submission is not an unhappy occasion at all. The publication process is part of the socialization of the text. When that text emerges as literary merchandise it will have been transformed by cultural forces into an artifact with nicks and scratches that do not need to be repaired. The blemishes might themselves be worthy of study. These editors do not see it as a duty to rescue the text from its previous editors or, to use an alternate figure, to purify the text from earlier corruption. To this group the moment of submission might be likened to watching one's child wave good-bye on the opening day of a first semester in college.

To a third group of scholarly editors, the moment of submission brings mixed feelings. One cannot predict what is about to happen to the text, but happen it must if the manuscript or typescript is to be transformed into a fully realized work of art. The text will be altered as it passes through the publication process. Some things will be lost, some gained; the work will be changed, perhaps irrevocably. For this group of editors, the moment of submission would be like watching a son or daughter enter into a first serious love affair.

It should be useful to explore what happens at this nexus, this moment at which the author submits a text to a publisher. Of chief concern is the matter of intention: how does it operate in the minds of those who will edit the author's work? Two questions present themselves:

1. At what point does the act of submission occur? Does it always take place when the author puts the text into the publisher's hands, or can it occur earlier?
2. Can an author delegate creative intention to a publisher? If so, how should the scholarly editor, viewing this act retrospectively, regard such a transfer of authority?

These questions arose frequently with the texts of Theodore Dreiser's novels *Sister Carrie* and *Jennie Gerhardt*. Throughout his career Dreiser worked closely with others in preparing his manuscripts and typescripts for publication. These people were not necessarily trade editors. Just as frequently they were personal editors whom Dreiser recruited or hired to assist him in typing, punctuating, revising, and cutting. For *Sister Carrie* his helpers were his wife, Sara Dreiser, and his friend Arthur Henry. For *Jennie Gerhardt* he again had help from his wife, but he quarreled with her over the cuts that she suggested in the text. The people with whom he eventually worked most closely on *Jennie Gerhardt* were trade editors at Harper and Brothers. For later writings he used a succession of people. Typically they were women; quite often they were his lovers as well as his editors. There were many such women in Dreiser's life: Sallie Kusell, Estelle Kubitz, Louise Campbell, and Marguerite Tjader are the best known. Some of them were more skilled and influential than others, but all played important roles in the making of various of his books.

Dreiser's usual practice was to turn over a holograph draft to his helper of the moment and ask her to copy it, or sometimes to "clean it up." The helper would make a typed copy of Dreiser's manuscript, correcting punctuation and spelling as she went and altering wording and style in small ways. She would leave blank spaces on the typescript whenever she could not decipher Dreiser's cramped handwriting and would correct obvious grammatical errors. Then she would often pencil in suggested cuts or revisions—sometimes minor, sometimes extensive—and give the typescript to Dreiser for his reactions. If he wanted a change to remain in the text he would leave it there; sometimes for cuts he would trace over the helper's excision marks in his own hand. If he did not approve of the changes he would erase them. Simultaneously he would do his own revising.

This appears to be a straightforward case of collaborative authorship. Dreiser was the dominant author whose name would go on the title page, but the published text would be the result of a collaboration. Dreiser was using helpers to catch stylistic, mechanical, and grammatical errors. One wonders whether this simple view is adequate, however, when one looks at the character of the changes. Most are routine enough—mechanical corrections or suggestions for eliminating infelicitous phrasing or clumsy syntax—but others bowdlerize or tone down the text. References to sexual desire, or simply to the human body, are removed. Passages critical of organized religion are softened or cut. Statements of bleak philosophical determinism are excised. Did Dreiser genuinely want these changes made in his text? One has passive evidence at least of his intentions—the penciled editorial alterations on the typescript, unerased and incorporated into the next typescript, which itself would go through this process of revision and retyping again. Several typescripts might be prepared and revised in this way before Dreiser would arrive at a final document to be presented to a publisher.

Did Dreiser let himself go in the drafting stages, knowing he would be rescued from his own excesses by his personal editors? Did he want the release of expressing sexual fantasy or nihilistic thinking without intending to publish what he had written? Conversely, did Dreiser long for freedom to express what he wrote in his drafts but become over the years a resigned, practical writer who *submitted* to laundering in order to publish in the literary marketplace of his time? These questions do not have precise answers, but scholarly editors must grapple with them all the same. They will be able to do so more successfully by readjusting their ideas about the act of submission.

Let's consider the final typescript produced by this method of composition. When that presentable form of the text was reached, and when Dreiser conveyed it to his publisher, was he at that moment submitting the literary work to the publication process? I believe that he was not, that in fact he had already submitted it when he handed it to his own helper some days or weeks before. I believe that Dreiser was using personal editors to help him anticipate what his publishers might require during the editing and proofing that were to come.

This is an important matter, however obvious it might appear to be, because it bears on the author's extended intentions. When Dreiser handed a manuscript or a revised typescript to Estelle Kubitz or Louise Campbell and asked her to clean it up, he was certainly delegating some portion of his authorial intention to his own editor. He was asking her to imagine her way into his mind so that she could perform the functions he might ideally have performed, had he the time or ability. Some of these were routine, such as the correction of misspellings and the addition of proper punctuation; others were harder, such as the elimination of clumsy syntax or the clarification of confusing passages. Others were more difficult still, such as the cutting and recasting of scenes. Dreiser's helper could operate freely because she knew that she was not the final authority. Dreiser himself would pass judgment on the performance, more or less closely, after the text had been handed back to him. If his helper had overstepped her bounds or done her tasks improperly, he could reject her revisions and suggestions.

Dreiser also seems to have been asking his personal editor to appropriate, ahead of time, some portion of the publisher's intentions. (Publishers have intentions in literary work, just as authors do.) Dreiser's helper was being asked to imagine her way into the minds of the trade editor and the head of the house, the persons to whom Dreiser's final typescript would be conveyed. There would be features of the text to which these people would probably object and for which they would want alterations or cuts. Dreiser's personal editor was being asked to anticipate these objections and to perform simultaneously in a quasi-collaborative and a quasi-adversarial role, as both author and publisher. The task of the scholarly editor therefore becomes mixed. This editor must attempt to disentangle the various motives under which Dreiser's helper was working and identify the different sets of extended and delegated intentions under which she was operating.

How would the three schools of editing I mentioned earlier be inclined to deal with this problem of delegated intention? The first school, the one which viewed the act of submission in a largely negative way, would probably disallow much of the work done by Dreiser's personal editors. His judgment would be seen as defective; the personal editors would be seen as interfering in the creative process. The original text would likely be restored, except for cases in which Dreiser's helper was correcting demonstrable mechanical errors, mistakes that would have to be emended identically by the scholarly editor.

The second group of scholarly editors would view the work done by Dreiser's personal editors as the initial step in the social construction or domestication of the text, a process necessary if that text were to be presented to its public. Nearly all of the changes suggested by Dreiser's helpers and subsequently approved by him would likely be incorporated into the reading text, not as emendations chosen by the scholarly editor but as features already present in a printed edition.

The third group of scholarly editors, among whom I count myself, would see the work of Dreiser's helpers as evidence of mixed intentions. Useful here are the terms employed by G. Thomas Tanselle in his article "The Editorial Problem of Final Authorial Intention."[1] Tanselle, borrowing from Michael Hancher, describes three kinds of intention: *programmatic, active,* and *final.*[2] *Programmatic* intention is the author's intention to create something—a plan to write and publish a sonnet, for example, or a novel. *Active* intention is the author's intention to be seen or understood as acting in a particular way. *Final* intention is the intention to make something happen—the hope that an essay or tale will change an audience's viewpoint about some subject, or, alternately, an expectation that the literary work will bring recognition and remuneration. Of the three, *active* intention is of greatest concern to the scholarly editor because it "concerns the meanings embodied in the work" (Tanselle, "Editorial Problem," 175).

Some of the changes made by Dreiser's personal editors did fulfill his active intentions. This work was done in the spirit of true collaboration; the alterations were approved by Dreiser and should be incorporated into a scholarly text. Others of the changes represent only a carrying forward of Dreiser's programmatic or final intentions. In order to incorporate these changes into a scholarly text, an editor would have to use some such argument as "It is what the author expected to see done to the text, either by the publisher or by others. The author had no choice, if he wanted to see the text published." Such changes should be disallowed, though they need to be recorded somewhere in a full-dress edition. The point is that a single editor, personal or trade, can be carrying forward two or three kinds of delegated intention simultaneously—programmatic, active, and final—in a single stint of work on a literary text or in a series of such stints.

The scholarly editor must take what is known about the author's life, professional career, and working habits, then add to it what can be learned about the publishing industry of the author's time and about the specific publishing houses and editors involved. From this evidence the editor can develop a set of standards by which to separate and classify the various sets of intentions at work in the minds of authors, editors, and publishers. The editor must then emend on the basis of these standards.

At the beginning of this paper I posed two questions. Suggested answers to them are as follows:

1. The act of submission can occur at any time during the compositional process. It does not necessarily occur when the author places a copy of the text in the publisher's hands. Often it occurs earlier.
2. Authors can delegate intention to personal editors and can encourage these editors to appropriate, imaginatively, the intentions of other persons—usually trade editors and publishers. Scholarly editors must seek to separate and classify the various sets of intentions at work; they must then develop strategies of emendation to help them choose which readings to allow into their texts and which to include in textual tables.

These answers generate a new set of questions, as follows:

1. Do authors, during the original act of composition, already seek to imagine their way into the minds of trade editors and publishers and to make choices accordingly? If so, is it wise, or even possible, for an editor to differentiate among authorial revisions as represented in original, unedited drafts, judging some to represent active intentions and others to represent programmatic or final intentions?
2. If an author delegates intention to a helper, is that intention not also delegated to the trade editor, though perhaps in lesser intensity? Trade

editors are not necessarily adversarial figures. Does the trade editor not function in almost the same way that the author's personal editor does?

3. Does the trade editor, like the author's personal editor, attempt to think forward into the minds of reviewers, public moralists, censors, and book buyers? Does the trade editor appropriate, imaginatively, their intentions as a guide?

4. Is the scholarly editor not appropriating authorial intention when editing the work years later? If so, then who warrants this appropriation? If the author's work is still in copyright, then those who control the literary estate must allow the scholarly editor to make the appropriation. If there is no literary estate, or if the writing is in the public domain, might it be said that the intellectual establishment bequeaths authorial intention to those who are qualified, by training and reputation, to exercise it?

5. How is a scholarly editor to develop a set of standards, a yardstick against which to measure the individual changes introduced into a text by these various persons? Is it advisable or possible to make such distinctions? Where does critical judgment leave off and personal taste take over? Is there any difference between the two?

Some examples will help to focus the discussion. The first two involve the revision of *Sister Carrie* by Dreiser's wife, Sara, and his friend Arthur Henry. This revision took place before the novel was submitted to Doubleday, Page and Co., its eventual publisher. Some of these alterations were made in the holograph of *Sister Carrie,* now at the New York Public Library; others were introduced into the typescript, now among Dreiser's papers at the Annenberg Rare Book and Manuscript Library, University of Pennsylvania.

In chapter 7 of the manuscript, Carrie's friend and eventual seducer, Charles Drouet, is attempting to persuade her not to return to her hometown. Drouet wishes her to stay in Chicago, where he will take care of her. Dreiser wrote this bit of dialogue for Drouet in the manuscript: "'What can you do back at Columbia City?' he went on, rousing by the words a picture of the dull world she had left in Carrie's mind." In Dreiser's handwritten draft, his wife relocated the awkwardly placed final prepositional phrase so that the end of the sentence now reads, "rousing by the words in Carrie's mind a picture of the dull world she had left" (68). Sara Dreiser's small revision removes possible confusion and does not interfere with artistic effect. It should be considered an extension of Dreiser's active intentions and be incorporated into the reading text, with an emendation entry indicating who was responsible for the change.

A second example involves revision by Arthur Henry on the setting-copy typescript. Carrie has by this point found her first job—a dull and soul-deadening position among coarse girls on an assembly line at a shoe factory. Carrie is taken to the foreman, who is told to show her what her tasks will be. Dreiser's original sentence in both manuscript and typescript reads, "He seemed rather annoyed at having to bother with such help, but put down her name and then led her across to where a line of girls were sitting on a line of stools in front of a line of clacking machines" (36). In typescript Arthur Henry revised to remove the repetition of "a line of." The last part of his condensed sentence reads, "across to where a line of girls occupied stools in front of clacking machines."[3] This reading appears on page 40 of the first edition. Did Dreiser approve the revision, or did he not notice it? Perhaps the revised sentence is an improvement, but has Henry not removed a verbal repetition that emphasizes the dull repetitiveness of the work? Did Dreiser consciously repeat "a line of" in order to make this point, or did he simply write a clumsy sentence which adventitiously mirrors the action he is describing? One cannot be sure, but if one is familiar with Dreiser's use of language and with the various forms of awkwardness his writing takes, one can say that this is not a typical form. Stylistic clumsiness in Dreiser's work is more a matter of word placement than of repetitiousness. I would conclude here that Dreiser used "a line of" three times in one sentence to create an effect. Henry's alteration was surely meant to help Dreiser, to extend Dreiser's active intentions; but the revision should be judged as a case of extended programmatic intention, an effort by Henry to remove what he believed to be verbal awkwardness and thus, in a small way, help conventionalize the language of the novel. The original repetitive wording should be preserved in the reading text; the rejection of Henry's revision would be handled by a *stet* note in the apparatus.

A second group of examples comes from the only surviving full typescript of *Jennie Gerhardt*. This document, housed in the Albert and Shirley Small Special Collections Library, University of Virginia, is a carbon typescript. Dreiser submitted the ribbon copy to Harper and Brothers in 1911. There it was heavily revised and cut by the trade editor Ripley Hitchcock and his subordinates. Their alterations were so extensive that a fresh typescript had to be prepared for the compositor. Extant correspondence and Dreiser's contract with Harper reveal that he was uneasy about this editorial work, but Hitchcock was pressing him for approval of the revised typescript so that typesetting could begin. Hitchcock wanted the novel to be ready for the fall 1911 bookselling season.

Dreiser allowed the altered text to be typeset, but he fought in proof for restoration of much of the cut material and succeeded in having some of it put back. Harper published the book on 19 October 1911.

Neither the ribbon typescript that Dreiser submitted to Harper nor the fresh setting-copy typescript made there survives today. The *typed* text of the carbon typescript in the C. Waller Barrett collection, however, preserves the text that Dreiser originally gave to Harper—minus, of course, whatever handwritten revisions he or his personal editors might have added on the ribbon copy before it was submitted. By collating the typed text on the carbon with the first printing of *Jennie Gerhardt,* one can discover what happened between typing and publication. Variants could have been introduced on Dreiser's ribbon typescript, on the Harper typescript, or in galleys or page proofs. Those responsible for introducing the changes could have been Dreiser and his personal editors, Hitchcock and his subordinates, or the compositors and proofreaders at the Harper printing plant. In editing *Jennie Gerhardt,* the problem was to differentiate individual variants, and classes of variants, one from another. What patterns of revision and cutting emerged? Who was likely responsible for them? Was the motivation active or programmatic? Which readings should be adopted for the Pennsylvania text, and which should be reported in the apparatus?

A good example occurs in chapter 20 of the carbon typescript. In this scene Lester Kane is negotiating with Jennie. She has agreed to be his mistress; in return he is to look after her nearly destitute family. The typescript text follows:

> "What is it, Jennie?" he asked helpfully. "You're so delicious. Can't you tell me?"
>
> Her hand was on the table. He reached over and laid his strong brown one on top of it.
>
> "I couldn't have a baby," she said finally and looked down.
>
> He looked at her and the charm of her frankness, her innate decency under conditions which were anomalous and compulsory, the simple unaffected recognition of the facts of life lifted her to a plane which she had not occupied before for him.
>
> "You're a great girl, Jennie," he said. "You're wonderful. But don't worry about that. **You don't need to. I understand a number of things that you don't yet.** It can be arranged. You don't need to have a child unless you want to, and I don't want to."

**He stopped and she opened her eyes in wonder and a kind of shame. She had never known that.**

He saw the question written on her face.

"It's so," he said. "You believe me, don't you? You think I know, don't you?"

"Yes," she faltered.

(Barrett typescript, 265–66)

The words in boldface above were cut between Dreiser's original typed text and the first edition. Also cut was a sentence a few lines later which reads, "She half wondered what it was he knew and how he could be so sure but he did not trouble to explain." In its place, the first edition reads, "Not for worlds could she have met his eyes" (165). These cuts and revisions remove references to Jennie's complete ignorance about birth control—a stunning lack of knowledge on her part, since she is by this point the mother of a child, a fact she is hiding from Lester. The choice here is not so simple. Did Dreiser make the cut or approve it because he did not want Jennie to appear so ignorant? Did he fear that readers would laugh at her naïveté? If so, then the cut could be seen as a carrying forward of his active intentions and should stand. But it might also be argued that Harper and Brothers would not have printed references to birth control, a controversial practice in 1911, when Margaret Sanger and other activists were risking public abuse and jail sentences for advocating the use of birth control devices.[4] The cuts, in this interpretation, were likely made by a nervous publisher's editor who was not collaborating with Dreiser in any sense. My decision for the Pennsylvania *Jennie Gerhardt* was to restore the cuts (see p. 158 of the edition). The passage is stronger for the restoration. Jennie's ignorance, the cause of many of the calamities that befall her, is made clear early in the novel.

A second example is taken from an earlier page of the Barrett typescript. Jennie has become pregnant with the child of Senator George Brander, who has died before he can marry her. Jennie carries the child to term, and as the hour of birth approaches the Gerhardt family doctor is brought in to officiate. The carbon typescript reads this way:

The doctor was curious to know who the father was and when informed lifted his eyes. "Indeed," he commented. "That ought to be a bright baby. **I think it will be a girl." He was judging from a peculiar conformation of the muscles of the back which at this period was to him**

**an invariable sign. "You need not worry," he said. "You will have an easy time. You are a strong girl." He tried to cheer the helpless family in other ways for he was a kind man.**

(Barrett typescript, 158)

The sentences in boldface were cut between Dreiser's typescript and the Harper first edition. There the passage ends with "bright baby." The doctor's prediction of the sex of the child has been removed, as have his reassurances to Jennie and her family.

The editor's decision here depends on an interpretation of the narrative voice. Is this omniscient narrator suggesting, in the uncut text, that the family doctor's method of predicting sex for an unborn child is trustworthy? If so, and if one is tempted to identify this narrative voice as Dreiser's, then was the cut made to protect Dreiser from appearing foolish? Would Dreiser have believed such nonsense? He grew up in a family that employed folk remedies and was an easy mark throughout his life for medical charlatans. If one puts this interpretation on the evidence (and I confess that it is an unlikely one), then the passage should be excluded from the text. The cut would be seen as an extension of Dreiser's active intentions, no matter who made it.

On the other hand, the narrative voice might be suggesting that the Gerhardt's family doctor, though kindly and well meaning, is little more than a quack. That implication would add to the depiction of the Gerhardts as people trapped by poverty, helpless before figures of authority. If one interprets the evidence in this way, then the cut cannot be seen as a part of Dreiser's active intentions. It must have been made to remove references to the body and to childbirth—an exercise of programmatic intention. There is indeed such a pattern of cutting in the entire text, a pattern consistent with the standards of trade publishers like Harper in the early 1900s. My own decision for the Pennsylvania *Jennie Gerhardt* was to disallow the cut and to restore the original full paragraph (96). Another editor, however, might make the opposite judgment. After all, the family doctor turns out to have been right: Jennie's baby is indeed a girl.

This approach to emendation places great responsibility on the scholarly editor. This editor's mind, knowledge, and standards are being substituted for the publication process to which the author first submitted the text. The text will now go through an improved publication process, more considerate of the author's intentions. An improved text, or at least a different one, will emerge.

Eclectic editing increases the critical and imaginative thinking needed to produce a scholarly text and makes it possible for two editors to address the same body of evidence and produce two quite different texts—especially when the revising is heavy. Scholarly editing of this kind is simultaneously an act of literary criticism and of biography. The editor employs interpretive skills in differentiating active from programmatic or final intentions and, in so doing, influences the later reading of the text by critics and teachers. At the same time the editor acts as a biographer, attempting to re-create human behavior from the surviving textual evidence and from the broader biographical portraits of the author that exist.

The development of such standards is difficult. Standards will vary from individual to individual. Some editors would argue that it is impossible to develop such standards or to follow them consistently; they are right, but what they advocate as an alternate course of action is tame. They would adhere to the received text and simply note who did what during the compositional process or, alternately, purge the text of virtually all nonauthorial alteration. Both of these approaches are plausible, and both are simpler because they are rigid. The other strategy—differentiation of variants, selective emendation, and the creation of an eclectic text—involves the frequent exercise of editorial judgment. I believe it to be the preferable course, certainly for Dreiser. Otherwise we read a text not so much written by him as simply approved by him, and often approved reluctantly. I would rather produce a text which is admittedly imperfect, but which has been restored to a form close to the one in which Dreiser might ideally have wanted to publish it.

NOTES

1. G. Thomas Tanselle, "The Editorial Problem of Final Authorial Intention," *Studies in Bibliography* 29 (1976): 167–211; also Tanselle, "Classical, Biblical, and Medieval Textual Criticism and Modern Editing," *Studies in Bibliography* 36 (1983), esp. 28, 49, 67. See in addition Noel Polk, *An Editorial Handbook for William Faulkner's "The Sound and the Fury"* (New York: Garland, 1985).

2. Michael Hancher, "Three Kinds of Intention," *Modern Language Notes* 87 (1972): 827–51.

3. A facsimile of this page of the typescript is included in James L. W. West III, *A "Sister Carrie" Portfolio* (Charlottesville: University Press of Virginia, 1985), 32.

4. See David M. Kennedy, *Birth Control in America: The Career of Margaret Sanger* (New Haven: Yale University Press, 1970); also *Margaret Sanger: An Autobiography* (New York: Norton, 1938).

# FAIR COPY, AUTHORIAL INTENTION, AND VERSIONING

The words *fair copy* are reassuring to a scholarly editor. The existence of a fair copy somewhere along the line of textual transmission gives the editor great moral authority. The editor can know that there once existed a copy of the text to which, for that moment, the author had applied the finishing touches. Even if this fair copy no longer survives, its one-time existence suggests that there is a tangible goal toward which an editor can strive or a hypothetical point from which to commence. The editor knows that the author directed careful attention to a single document and got it "just right." Then and only then was the work submitted to the publication process.

The mental image of a fair copy conveyed to a publisher in a ceremonial act has probably been attractive to scholarly editors because most of them are teachers, and all of them have been students. Submitting a fair copy of a poem or novel to a publisher is rather like turning in the final copy of a term paper to a professor. The assumption by the pedagogue is that this is the student's best work. The student has worked hard on the document and finally, in the wee hours of the morning, has said, "There! I'm done! This copy is just the way I want it."

Authors, most of whom have also been students, probably think in the same fashion, especially during the early stages of their careers. They prepare copies of literary works which suit them in all details; they place these copies on the desk and say, with satisfaction, "Voila! Finished!" Of course even the most inexperienced author knows that the work is not really finished, but paradoxically this imparts even more authority to the fair copy. Its creation has been a private act about which the author can say, "For now, this once, without interference, I have created an incarnation of this text to suit myself." The fair copy represents the best that the author can do; it embodies what is intended for the literary work at that time and in that place. It is the final copy of the term paper, meant to be submitted not to a professor but to an authority figure with much greater power—a publisher.

For some literary works this description of fair copy is valid. The author did apply the final touches to a single copy of the text and did convey it to the publisher with the stated or implied message "This is the way I want it." Behavior such as this usually occurs early in the author's career; one often finds it in the compositional history of first novels. The writer has no publisher or contract and must shop the manuscript about. The writer must put the best foot forward—must dot the i's, cross the t's, and "submit clean copy." Years later, when this first novel has attained the status of a classic, a scholarly editor can plan an entire strategy around the fair copy. Its existence at some point in the making of the work clarifies immensely the question of intention.

What I will examine here, however, are cases in which this scenario was not played out. These are instances in which there was never a fair copy and never a formal act or ceremony of submission. For such works, fair copy existed only in some blurry, in-between region of intention, midway between the transmission of an unfinished form of the text to the publisher and the emergence of that text, some months later, as a printed artifact. This changes things considerably. It makes it much more difficult for an editor to create an ideal text, if that is the goal, and it requires a different way of thinking about intention and the compositional process.

As examples I will use fair copies prepared by three modern American novelists: Theodore Dreiser, F. Scott Fitzgerald, and Ernest Hemingway. Their practices will no doubt remind readers of the compositional habits of other authors in other periods. Dreiser, Fitzgerald, and Hemingway prepared fair copies very carefully for their early novels. Later, when they were settled in comfortable relationships with publishers and had some leverage, they were much less apt to prepare fair copies, submitting instead unfinished documents and bringing them to completion in collaboration with publishers.

Dreiser prepared fair-copy typescripts of his first two novels, *Sister Carrie* and *Jennie Gerhardt*. He had a typescript made of *Sister Carrie*, polished it, submitted it to Harper and Brothers in the spring of 1900, had it rejected, cut and revised it further, and submitted it to Doubleday, Page and Co., where it eventually served as setting copy for the first edition. But Dreiser learned that the text of *Sister Carrie* was far from being fixed or stable in his fair-copy typescript. The text was bowdlerized and altered in numerous ways on the typescript itself and was changed further in proof. To the publisher, Dreiser learned, his carefully revised typescript was simply a point from which to begin making alterations.

Dreiser finished his second novel, *Jennie Gerhardt,* in the spring of 1911. He had a fair-copy typescript prepared, submitted it to Macmillan, had it rejected, submitted it to Harper and Brothers, and had it accepted. This time the fair copy proved to be even less sacrosanct. Harper editor Ripley Hitchcock and several subeditors under his direction almost completely rewrote the novel for print, making so many alterations on the fair copy that they had to have a fresh typescript made for the compositor. Dreiser's fair copy was so covered with editorial changes that Hitchcock was reluctant to let him see it and had to be prodded, by Dreiser's literary agent, to allow the author to examine it. Dreiser objected to much of the cutting and alteration of *Jennie Gerhardt* and succeeded in having some material restored before publication, but he was still unhappy about what had been done to the book and was worried that the Harper editors had cut too deeply.

For all his irritation, Dreiser had learned a lesson about fair copy. A fair copy took much time, energy, and thought to prepare. A great deal of that effort was likely to be wasted. At this point in his career Dreiser had set himself the hellishly difficult task of turning out a new novel every six months. He seems to have realized, perhaps with a sigh of relief, that at least he would not have to prepare fair copies for these projected novels. If the publisher's editors were going to cut, rewrite, and repunctuate the text, they why not allow them to do this work, and other mechanical work as well, especially if it were part of the service? For Dreiser it now became a question of how much labor he could shift from his own shoulders, or those of his assistants, to the shoulders of the publisher.

One can see the results of Dreiser's thinking in the preparation of the text of his next novel, *The Financier,* published by Harper in 1912. Dreiser produced a holograph that was not a first draft but was not exactly a fair copy either. Evidences of several layers of work survive in this handwritten document: page-numbering sequences that indicate additions and cuts, lengthy bridge passages, and leaves on which the writing ends midfolio and midsentence, indicating revision and splicing. Dreiser must have invested a good deal of labor in this longhand draft, but it is not a true fair copy. Punctuation is haphazard and spelling erroneous, some passages are in need of clarification, and there are inconsistencies in chronology and characterization.

Dreiser gave this document in batches to Ripley Hitchcock at Harper. His implied message could not have been "This is precisely the way I want it."

The message must have been more nearly "You take it from here for a while; I'll come back later, and we'll work toward the printed text together." This is in fact how *The Financier* was produced. Hitchcock had a typescript made at the Harper offices, and he and his subeditors cut and revised it. Dreiser, who had been traveling in Europe, then reentered the compositional process, and together he and the Harper editors brought the first edition into being. Dreiser was learning to co-opt the publisher's energy and resources; he was also sparing himself the effort of preparing a fair copy and the irritation that would come when the text of his fair copy was not respected.[1]

Does this change the way one would prepare a scholarly edition of *The Financier?* Without a true fair copy, a text brought by Dreiser to a point of stasis, how should one proceed? I suggest that an editor would still be able to use Dreiser's holograph as a base text, but that the editor's attitude toward emendations adopted from later forms of the text would need to change. With both *Sister Carrie* and *Jennie Gerhardt,* one could view variants between fair copy and first print with some suspicion. Dreiser created fair copies of these works; he brought their texts to settled points, so far as he was concerned. His fair copies can therefore be treated as beginning points in the editorial process, and their authority is strong enough that an editor can justify efforts to guard their readings against later alteration. With *The Financier* the holograph does not possess this same authority. One would have to be more liberal in one's attitude toward the publisher's (and the author's) changes between holograph and print, so far as these could be identified and differentiated from one another. The dials on the "intention machine" would have to be adjusted to allow more revisions and cuts from the first printing to be emended back into the base text.[2]

A similar pattern applies for F. Scott Fitzgerald. He created fair copies in typescript of his first two novels, *This Side of Paradise* (1920) and *The Beautiful and Damned* (1922). These differ from Dreiser's first novels in that they were not significantly cut or bowdlerized by Fitzgerald's publisher, Charles Scribner's Sons. For his third novel Fitzgerald, working mostly in France, created a fair-copy typescript which he tentatively entitled *Trimalchio* and sent to his editor at Scribner's, Maxwell Perkins. In a letter of response, Perkins praised *Trimalchio* but made suggestions for revision that prompted Fitzgerald to restructure and significantly revise his novel in galleys. Fitzgerald also changed his title to *The Great Gatsby.* Fitzgerald trusted Perkins to see this revised text through to publication. There was no time for Fitzgerald, in France, to receive and return a second set of proofs. (Also, one suspects, Perkins did not want to give Fitzgerald a second shot at the text, fearing even more extensive revisions.) Perkins supervised the resetting of type and had the novel given a careful in-house proofreading. It was published on 10 April 1925. Here it can be argued that Fitzgerald submitted two fair copies—*Trimalchio* in typescript and *The Great Gatsby* in revised galleys.

But for Fitzgerald's fourth novel, *Tender Is the Night*, no fair copy ever existed. The composition of this novel spanned a period of nine years, many of them troubled years for Fitzgerald and his wife, Zelda. He fell into debt with Scribner's and had no easy way of repaying his publisher. In a gesture meant partly to ease Fitzgerald's financial burdens, Scribner's offered to serialize *Tender Is the Night* in *Scribner's Magazine* for a payment of fifteen thousand dollars, which was to be counted against Fitzgerald's outstanding balance with the house. Fitzgerald accepted the offer. He had not completed the composition of the novel when he and Scribner's made this agreement. Thus when the first of four installments of *Tender Is the Night* began appearing in *Scribner's Magazine* in January 1934, Fitzgerald had not yet finished composing the latter parts of his text. He submitted fair copy to the magazine for the first installments, read and revised proofs of these magazine segments, and continued working in holograph and typescript on the later chapters of his book.

In order to have the trade edition ready for the bookshops shortly after the last segment of the magazine serial had appeared, Scribner's now had their typesetters compose the early chapters of the clothbound edition. At certain points Fitzgerald was reading book proofs for these early chapters while simultaneously composing and revising copy for the final magazine installments. This must have been a difficult juggling act. Some documents, both typescripts and proofs, appear to have been discarded and are no longer extant. As a consequence there does not survive today a continuous fair copy of *Tender Is the Night*. In preparing the serial and book texts for print, Fitzgerald likely never thought that preparation of a fair copy was necessary.

Hemingway's attitude toward fair copy follows a similar progression. He appears to have invested much time and energy in the preparation of fair copies for his first two novels, *The Sun Also Rises* (1926) and *A Farewell to Arms* (1929). His method is of some interest: in both cases he had a ribbon and at least one carbon copy made of the text, then submitted one of the carbons to his publisher (also Charles Scribner's Sons) to serve as setting copy. Meanwhile Hemingway retained the ribbon copy and entered final revisions on it, as he reread the text from time to time. This ribbon copy was, in effect, his fair copy, though he never submitted it to his publisher. When galleys arrived,

Hemingway transferred most of his late revising and polishing from the ribbon typescripts to the proofs. To judge from his markings on the galleys for both novels, he apparently decided against some of his ribbon-copy revisions, once the typeset text was in front of him, or decided to execute different revisions of passages which had dissatisfied him during some earlier rereading. And of course he made other, independent alterations while reading the galleys.

This was an elaborate process. It suggests that Hemingway cared a great deal about his text. One can therefore understand his frustration when he found out that the editors at Scribner's were going to take many liberties, large and small, with his words and punctuation. His narratives were going to be cut, bowdlerized, and thoroughly restyled in accidentals.[3] Hemingway learned that Maxwell Perkins, who was also his editor, often would not turn his full attention to a book until after its text had been typeset. Perkins could afford this luxury because Scribner's operated its own printing plant, which was more responsive (and less expensive) than jobbers would have been. Hemingway therefore seems to have decided that if Perkins were going to treat the setting copy as no more than an intermediate stage and were not going to examine it carefully, then Hemingway might as well do the same, withholding his own full attention from the text until it was set in type.

One sees evidence of this shift in tactics with *Death in the Afternoon* (1932).[4] Hemingway inscribed a handwritten manuscript, had it typed, and produced a second draft that was a composite of the initial typescript leaves, plus numerous holograph additions. He had this second draft typed up, but he was far from finished with the text. He revised this new typescript heavily in his own hand and then, without having it retyped, sent it to Scribner's. Galleys were set from this hand-revised typescript. Only then did Hemingway and Perkins get down to real work—in the galleys, where major alterations were made. Fortunately all of these stages of the text are extant, either at the John F. Kennedy Presidential Library in Boston, where the bulk of Hemingway's papers are housed, or at the Harry Ransom Humanities Research Center at the University of Texas. It will therefore be possible for an editor some day to identify who did what to *Death in the Afternoon* at every stage of its development. The text toward which an eclectic editor might strive never came close to existing as a fair copy. It existed only in the abstract, somewhere between the typescript Hemingway sent to Scribner's and the published book that he and Perkins caused to appear.

As with *The Financier* and *Tender Is the Night*, this will affect a scholarly editor's thinking and procedures. The base text for a critical edition of *Death in the Afternoon* should probably be the revised typescript which Hemingway sent to Scribner's, but in line with Hemingway's own attitude this typescript should not be treated with the same respect that one would accord a true fair copy. The text aimed for in an eclectic edition would instead exist somewhere between that typescript and the text of the first edition.[5]

Situations such as these will create problems for an editor committed to the technique of versioning. The essence of versioning is to publish incarnations of a work of literature from various points in its textual history. No synthesis is attempted, no eclectic or ideal text aimed for. Each version of the text is thought to possess some authority, and the entire literary work exists in a continuum, from early through intermediate to late versions. Together these versions possess a collective final authority.

This approach works well for prose narratives such as Richard Wright's autobiographical *Black Boy / American Hunger.* Wright began composing the book sometime in 1943 under the title "Black Confession." In December 1943 he gave a finished typescript to his agent, Paul Revere Reynolds. This version, entitled "American Hunger," was divided into two sections—"Southern Night," telling the story of Wright's years in the American South up to 1927, and "The Horror and the Glory," treating his experiences after he moved to Chicago in 1927 and joined the Communist Party there. Reynolds submitted Wright's typescript to Edward C. Aswell, a senior editor at Harper and Brothers, and Aswell accepted it for publication in January 1944.

Aswell had *American Hunger* typeset, and together he and Wright brought it to final page proofs by May. During that process Aswell, fearing criticism for obscenity, asked Wright to compose substitute lines for a short passage in which he had referred to the sexual organs of black males. (A white co-worker says to the quasi-autobiographical character called Richard, "I heard that a nigger can stick his prick in the ground and spin around on it like a top.") Wright agreed to the bowdlerization and wrote an alternate passage.

Aswell now submitted bound page proofs of *American Hunger* to Book-of-the-Month Club. BOMC agreed to take the book—an enormous windfall of money and publicity for Wright—but asked that Wright shorten the narrative by lopping off all of "The Horror and the Glory," the second section of the book, comprising almost one-third of its text. Surely Wright was ambivalent about making such a major cut, but in the event he decided to accept the book-club offer and shorten the text. Working with Dorothy Canfield Fisher, one of the BOMC judges, he wrote a new ending of around fourteen hundred words for "Southern Night." He also changed the title of his book to

*Black Boy.* It was published under that title in the spring of 1945 and enjoyed spectacularly good sales and reviews, quickly becoming a major document in twentieth-century African American literature. Wright published some of the sections from "The Horror and the Glory" in the *Atlantic Monthly, Mademoiselle,* and *Cross Section* in 1944 and 1945; but the full text of the section did not appear until 1977, seventeen years after his death, in a slim volume from Harper and Row entitled *American Hunger*—the old title. By then the 1945 text of *Black Boy* had reached canonical status.

The two parts of *American Hunger* were finally brought together in a cloth-bound edition by the Library of America in 1991; a HarperPerennial paperback of this text appeared in 1993 and is still in print today. These texts, though they do not announce it, were edited using principles derived from versioning. The text of the Library of America / HarperPerennial edition was typeset from the May 1944 page proofs of the original *American Hunger,* a text to which, as we have seen, Wright had given his approval at a fixed point in time. The section titles "Southern Night" and "The Horror and the Glory" were restored, along with the passage that Aswell had caused to be bowdlerized. Thus readers and critics could for the first time encounter Wright's text as he originally wrote it and see how complex and experimental a book it was in his initial conception. And by using the textual notes and apparatus for these editions of *American Hunger,* readers could still reconstruct *Black Boy* and could also read the substitute passage that Wright prepared for the apprehensive Aswell.

Teachers and critics of American literature have been coming to terms with *American Hunger.* In its 1945 version *Black Boy* is a powerful book, connected closely with nineteenth-century slave narratives that tell of escape from the benighted South. The ending written for the 1945 text, if not optimistic, at least implies that the move north to Chicago will allow Wright to escape most racial oppression and social discrimination, which seems to be located only in the South. The restored *American Hunger* makes it clear that there is no escape from racial discrimination in American society, north or south. Wright is as heavily oppressed in Chicago as he was in Mississippi, though the discrimination is now covert and comes from sources other than institutionalized segregation. It comes from his own family, traditional religion, white northerners, and the Communist Party. In expanded form *American Hunger* also reveals itself more clearly as a book written in the naturalist tradition, influenced strongly by Dreiser and H. L. Mencken, both of whom Wright acknowledged as models.

Versioning is an attractive approach for anyone who has ever prepared an eclectic edition, but the technique is not flexible enough to be applied successfully in all situations. An inherent assumption of versioning is that each surviving embodiment of the text possesses some measure of finality. It must be a text to which either the author, or the author plus the publisher, has at some point applied final approval. This can happen more than once in the history of the text, as with *Trimalchio* and *The Great Gatsby*. Versioning will probably work for such novels as *Sister Carrie* and *Jennie Gerhardt*, or for *The Sun Also Rises* and *A Farewell to Arms*, but it will not work for books like *The Financier, Tender Is the Night*, and *Death in the Afternoon*. The versions of these works that survive are not sufficiently final, or "fair," to be of much use or interest if reproduced. And the same problem crops up in subsequent books by both Dreiser and Hemingway—Dreiser's *The Titan* (1914), for example, and Hemingway's *To Have and Have Not* (1937).

The technique of versioning is easier to apply to short or midlength lyric poems than to novels or other long prose works. Poems can be published or facsimiled in many versions and can be compared and discussed at length. Numerous successive published versions of lyric poems do often survive— periodical, first book, collected edition, newly revised collected edition, deathbed edition. Versioning would not be realistic, however, for long and marginally significant works such as *The Financier*, at 780 pages in its first edition, or for *Death in the Afternoon* at 517. Nor is photo-facsimile or digital publication really a workable approach. The holograph of *The Financier* is 1,663 pages in length. The relevant materials for *Death in the Afternoon* occupy over five hundred leaves of archival material, rather too many to be reproduced for this less-than-major work by Hemingway.

Versioning is a good editorial technique for short writings that survive in multiple published forms (each of which can be thought to possess some measure of finality) or for longer works that exist in clearly discrete texts. But for Dreiser, Fitzgerald, and Hemingway, at least, versioning is not an attractive alternative for long, minor works which exist before publication only in intermediate, unsettled texts or in published versions produced in sometimes vexed collaborations with trade houses. Opportunities to edit lengthy works of prose, in fully funded editions, do not arise with great frequency. If publisher and money are in place, one cannot dodge one's responsibility and opt for versioning as an editorial technique. One should apply editorial judgment to the surviving drafts, with or without a fair copy, and create an eclectic text.

NOTES

1. For an account of the complexities of composition, see James M. Hutchisson, "The Creation (and Reduction) of *The Financier,*" *Papers on Language and Literature* 27 (Spring 1991): 243–59. I am not addressing here a separate set of questions that relate to Dreiser's revised edition of *The Financier,* published by Boni and Liveright in 1927.

2. This is the approach taken by the editors of *The Financier: The Critical Edition,* ed. Roark Mulligan; gen. ed., Thomas P. Riggio (Urbana: University of Illinois Press, 2010). Page proofs of the 1912 first edition were selected as copy-text, and much material cut by Dreiser on the advice of others was restored. The Illinois Dreiser edition is the successor to the Pennsylvania Dreiser edition.

3. See Frederic Joseph Svoboda, *Hemingway and "The Sun Also Rises"* (Lawrence: University of Kansas Press, 1983); Michael S. Reynolds, *Hemingway's First War: The Making of "A Farewell to Arms"* (Princeton: Princeton University Press, 1976); Reynolds, "Words Killed, Wounded, Missing in Action," *Hemingway Notes* 6 (Spring 1981): 2–9; Scott Donaldson, "Censorship and *A Farewell to Arms,*" *Studies in American Fiction* 19 (Spring 1991): 85–93.

4. See the study by Robert W. Lewis, "The Making of *Death in the Afternoon,*" in *Ernest Hemingway: The Writer in Context,* ed. James Nagel (Madison: University of Wisconsin Press, 1984), 31–52.

5. Problems with fair copy exist also in William Faulkner's texts (especially the later ones) and have been addressed by Noel Polk, the editor of Faulkner's novels for the Library of America series. For an analysis of fair copy for Faulkner, see the introduction and the chapter "Where the Comma Goes" in Polk's *Children of the Dark House: Text and Context in Faulkner* (Jackson: University Press of Mississippi, 1996): vii–xv, 3–21.

# ALCOHOL AND DRINKING IN *SISTER CARRIE*

Is alcohol a factor in *Sister Carrie?* Is it important in any of Dreiser's writings? He made no serious effort that I'm aware of in his books and articles to explore the effects of drinking on human behavior. Perhaps he felt unqualified; probably the subject didn't interest him in the same way that it did Fitzgerald and Hemingway and Malcolm Lowry and William Styron—and many other writers who have explored alcohol and alcoholism. Dreiser's characters are driven by forces and compulsions other than drink, most of them economic and social. Lester Kane in *Jennie Gerhardt,* for example, dies in part from overindulgence in rich foods and wines, but there is no suggestion that he is an alcoholic. He expires more from weariness with life and bafflement over its meaning than from any addiction. And no one important in the Trilogy of Desire or *An American Tragedy* or the other fiction or nonfiction is destroyed by drinking.

The same can be said, for the most part, of *Sister Carrie.* If ever a man had reason to turn to liquor for solace, George Hurstwood would be that man, especially after he bottoms out in New York City. Certainly liquor has been a part of his life; he manages two saloons in the course of the novel, and he must know that liquor can be soothing and can help a man to forget his past. But there is no hint that Hurstwood is a drinker; he is destroyed by economic and social forces, not by bad personal habits. Likewise with Drouet, who seems to enjoy a glass from time to time, but who is energized by the pursuit of women, not by the bottle.

There are, however, three passages concerning alcohol in *Sister Carrie,* present together only in the Pennsylvania text of the novel, that are important. These passages are the subject of this essay. I want to argue that in Dreiser's original conception of *Sister Carrie* these passages constitute a pattern, a leitmotif that is used to measure the three principal male characters. Two of these passages are not present in the first edition, the 1900 Doubleday, Page and Co.

text, but were restored to the 1981 edition of the novel from the University of Pennsylvania Press. The third is present in the 1900 edition *and* the Pennsylvania text. Dreiser removed one passage from the typescript of the novel, probably between the time he submitted it to Harper in May 1900 and had it turned down and the time a few weeks later when he sent it to Doubleday. The other passage vanished between the setting-copy typescript and the first printing. In preparing the Pennsylvania text, I restored those two passages, reasoning that the cuts were made either to take out references to liquor or simply to move the plot along more swiftly. I'd like now to reexamine my thinking in making those restorations and to speculate about how the novel is changed by the presence or absence of the passages.

All three passages about drinking occur within a space of about one hundred pages. The first occurs just after Drouet has discovered that Carrie has been seeing Hurstwood in the afternoons. He goes to their apartment, resolved to confront her with his new knowledge. "The drummer was flushed and excited, and full of great resolve to know all about her relations with Hurstwood," wrote Dreiser in his manuscript. Then comes this detail: "He had taken several drinks and was warm for his purpose" (223).

Drouet proceeds to make a fool of himself. He tells Carrie that Hurstwood is a married man, something she has not known, and she, in a display of emotional illogic, becomes angry with him for not telling her about Hurstwood's matrimonial status. Drouet does not mean to break off with Carrie; he does not suspect her of serious wrongdoing. His vanity has been wounded, and he wants to reassert control over her. To his surprise, however, she shows considerable spunk. "I won't talk about it," she says. "Whatever has happened is your own fault" (232). Drouet, after whining a little, packs some things in a valise and puts his hand on the doorknob. "You can go to the deuce as far as I am concerned," he says in his exit line. "I'm no sucker" (232).

This is an important scene. It sets in motion all else that will happen in the novel. Hurstwood, who has been observed riding in a buggy with Carrie, is facing problems of his own now—an angry, unforgiving wife who is dictating severe financial terms for a divorce settlement. He will shortly steal ten thousand dollars from his employers, lure Carrie (now alone) onto a train to Montreal, and progress from there to New York City with her. It's necessary that Drouet behave foolishly when he confronts Carrie. Certainly those "several drinks" he has taken, in Dreiser's original conception of the scene, would have muddled his judgment. Was Dreiser trying to suggest that Drouet was not foolish enough on his own to botch this showdown with Carrie? Did the drummer need assistance from alcohol?

It's impossible to know exactly what Dreiser was thinking. What we do know is that the sentence quoted above ("He had taken several drinks and was warm for his purpose.") is present on page 264 of the setting-copy typescript but is missing from page 242 of the first printing. It must therefore have been cut in galleys or page proofs. But who made the cut? Perhaps it was made by someone at Doubleday, Page and Co. It might have been made by Dreiser, either under pressure from the publisher or at the suggestion of someone else or of his own volition. We do know that Dreiser removed references to sex and instances of mild profanity and blasphemy from the typescript at the publisher's prompting. These passages were queried in blue pencil; Dreiser responded by making the excisions.[1] Might this process have extended into the galley and page-proof stages, where this reference to Drouet's drinking was targeted? We also know that Dreiser was influenced to make cuts and changes before publication by Arthur Henry, his friend, and Sara White Dreiser, his wife. Some of these changes toned down potentially offensive passages. Might one of these two persons have suggested that he cut the sentence about Drouet's drinking from the galleys or page proofs?

These are possible explanations, but let's assume for now that Dreiser made the cut himself, without pressure or prompting. Why might he have done so? Possibly he did not want Drouet to have alcohol as an excuse. Drouet is goodhearted but shallow. He is not long on intellect, nor is he the sort of man who would handle himself nimbly in a face-off with an angry woman. Perhaps Dreiser wanted to take alcohol out of this equation and let Drouet make a fool of himself without having taken those "several drinks." That sounds plausible, but it's no more demonstrable than the other two propositions.[2]

The next mention of alcohol in *Sister Carrie* is the one that remains unchanged from manuscript to typescript to published book. This reference occurs in the important scene in which Hurstwood, depressed over his problems with his wife, begins drinking with some patrons at the saloon he manages—several actors, a theatrical manager, and a wealthy rounder of Chicago. Hurstwood joins in the drinking "right heartily" and matches his companions "glass for glass." Dreiser notes, "It was not long before the imbibing began to tell" (266). Lubricated by liquor, the men begin telling droll stories of sexual conquests. Hurstwood contributes a few of his own, and they continue drinking.

When closing time comes at midnight, Hurstwood is "in a very roseate state." His mind, Dreiser tells us, is "warm in its fancies" (266). He retires to his office, counts up the receipts, and discovers the ten thousand dollars in the safe. In these sections, Dreiser reminds us twice more that Hurstwood is still under the influence of drink. "Wine was in his veins," we are told (268). And then, about a page farther on, "The imbibation of the evening had not yet worn off. . . . [He] was still flushed with the fumes of liquor" (269). Hurstwood's reason is beclouded when he takes the money. He loses his head, puts the cash into his satchel, watches the door to the safe close and click shut, then panics and runs.

Dreiser removed none of these references to alcohol between manuscript and typescript or between typescript and print. He must have felt that Hurstwood, normally a man of probity if not actual honesty, would have needed a prod from alcohol to commit an act of thievery. Dreiser was providing an explanation for Hurstwood's bad judgment. Whatever Dreiser's apprehensions (if he had any) about referring to alcohol in his text, he must have felt that these references needed to stay. It's also true that these sentences would have been difficult to remove. There are several of them scattered throughout a lengthy scene; they are integral to the language and motivation of the section. Dreiser would have had to rewrite from scratch in order to remove the mentions of drinking.

The third reference to alcohol also comes in an important scene—the one in which Carrie goes to dinner at Sherry's restaurant with Mr. and Mrs. Vance and Robert Ames. This is Carrie's introduction to Ames, and ours as well. Ames will play an important part in what is to come. He will function as a tutor of sorts for Carrie, setting an example that she will attempt to follow. The portly, prosperous Mr. Vance spreads himself in the elegant restaurant, ordering "freely of soup, oysters, roast meats and side dishes." Vance, Dreiser tells us, also has "several bottles of wine brought, which were set down beside the table in a wicker basket." Then follows this exchange:

> Young Ames volunteered the information that they knew he did not drink.
> "I don't care for wine either," said Carrie.
> "You poor things," said Mrs. Vance. "You don't know what you're missing. You ought to drink a little, anyhow."
> "No," said Carrie, "I don't believe I will." (333)

Ames does not use alcohol; this is almost the first thing we learn about him. Carrie, watching him refuse the wine, decides on the spot to follow his lead, the first of several times she will do so in the chapters that follow. The small exchange begs for interpretation, not least because Ames is generally thought to be Dreiser's representative in *Sister Carrie*. The exterior details of his life are probably taken from the career of the inventor Thomas Edison, but the ideas and the personality seem to be Dreiser's—as Dreiser wanted to see himself. Ames, like Dreiser, is not interested in drink. He will speak with a voice unbefuddled by alcohol. He will operate with reason and speak with clarity.

About one hundred pages earlier we have seen Drouet, in the Pennsylvania text, make a fool of himself under the influence of whiskey. About fifty pages after that, Hurstwood has made an even bigger mess of his affairs after drinking too much. Ames stands in contrast to Drouet and Hurstwood. He is more intelligent and independent than they, much less dazzled by wealth and material display, infinitely better read and informed, more intuitive and sympathetic toward Carrie. In the Pennsylvania text, he has announced that he does not drink alcohol, a trait Carrie seems to like and which she mimics. Is his abstinence another instance of his superiority to Drouet and Hurstwood?

The exchange about wine at Sherry's, however, was cut from the typescript (389) by Dreiser and does not appear in the Doubleday text (355). And here we do have evidence that someone else suggested the cut to Dreiser, who then made it. We know from Dreiser's later testimony that Henry went through the typescript of *Sister Carrie* and marked passages that he thought could be pruned. Evidence of Henry's work survives in the left-hand margins of the setting-copy typescript sheets. He drew lines bracketing the passages that he recommended for excision, and Dreiser came behind and made the cuts, sometimes (but not always) erasing Henry's lines. On this particular typescript sheet, Henry's marks were erased but are still easily visible around the passage in which Ames and Carrie turn down the wine. It's likely that Henry suggested the cut before Dreiser made it.

One's best guess is that Arthur Henry failed to recognize the point Dreiser was making about alcohol (if indeed he was making such a point) and saw the small exchange about wine as a bit of detail that could be dispensed with. From his other work on the typescript it's fair to say that Henry was trying to streamline the narrative. Dreiser went ahead and made the cut; we can only speculate about *his* motives. Perhaps he had decided that the point about alcohol was not important. Perhaps he had forgotten the contrast that I believe he was making between Drouet and Hurstwood on the one hand and Ames on the other. Perhaps he was overly trusting of Henry's judgment. (He cut almost every passage that Henry marked for removal.) Or perhaps he had no point at all to make about the drinking habits of these three men. It is impossible finally to know.

It should be obvious what has been going on here. I have been constructing small narratives and deploying literary interpretations to explain the presence of alcohol in three places in *Sister Carrie*. These narratives provide explanations for Dreiser's removal of two of those references. I have wanted to find reasons that will justify my having restored those references to the Pennsylvania text. Perhaps I should say that *we* have been constructing such narratives, for I would guess that readers of this essay have been doing the same thing as they have followed these speculations, perhaps inventing some alternate motivations for Dreiser or constructing some other interpretations of his text. This is fun. It's what textual editors do. At base it's an exercise in biography. It is certainly not a dispassionate consideration of flat textual evidence—not a turn-the-crank exercise in editorial method. It's a mixture of biography, textual scholarship, and literary interpretation.

I won't spin out the implications of these passages any further, but I encourage readers to do so. It seems to me, in looking back now over thirty years to the late 1970s, when I was first trying to make decisions about what to restore to Dreiser's text and what not to restore, that my evidence for restoring the reference to Drouet's "several drinks" was thin and speculative. That doesn't mean that the decision was wrong, only that I took a leap of faith in putting the sentence back into the text. I did so because I conceived of Doubleday, Page and Co. as keen to remove as much disreputable behavior as possible from *Sister Carrie* and of Dreiser as willing to go along a certain distance in order to mollify the publisher. The year, after all, was 1900, and representatives of the genteel tradition were very much in the saddle in the literary world—as editors, book critics, and publishers. Temperance was a large issue in American society. Temperance advocates watched popular literature closely and attacked authors and their publishers if works of fiction were favorable or neutral on the subject of alcohol. Dreiser, with his experience in the magazine world, would have known this. Perhaps in such an atmosphere Drouet's "several drinks" could be left out. I also restored the reference to Drouet's drinking because I liked the three-part statement about alcohol. Drouet drinks and behaves foolishly; Hurstwood drinks and behaves irrationally; Ames does not drink and behaves admirably if a bit stiffly. I thought I discerned a pattern, a statement that Dreiser wanted to make, but I could have been wrong.

I was on firmer ground, I believe, in restoring the lines in which Ames turns down the wine at Sherry's and Carrie follows suit. This is just the sort of small touch that Dreiser was good at. It is also the kind of detail that Henry wanted Dreiser to cut at other points in the typescript. The restoration of such material to the Pennsylvania *Sister Carrie* makes it a richer, more suggestive and allusive novel than the Doubleday text. Here I have not only my interpretation to rely on but also Henry's marks in the margins, bracketing the passage for removal.

Textual editing of this kind is not a mechanical process. It requires an editor to think of *Sister Carrie* as an unstable, unsettled text, capable of yielding many variations in interpretation, especially when one knows the origins and textual history of important passages. A game of "What if?" is instructive here. What if the reference to Drouet's drinking were absent but the reference to Ames's abstinence were present? A textual editor could justify such a course. One's opinion of Drouet might change: he might seem even more of a fool (because he is sober and still behaves in a silly way), and Ames might seem simply to be a stuffed shirt who cannot relax and enjoy himself with a little wine at dinner. Or what if, as in the Doubleday text, only Hurstwood drinks and no mention is made of Drouet's "several drinks" or of Ames's refusal to imbibe? In that case the novel might be seen to contain a veiled moral lesson: if one takes alcohol before making important decisions, one risks ruin and destruction. Or what if, as in the Pennsylvania text, alcohol is present in all three places? Here Dreiser is asking us to judge these three men, all of whom are important in Carrie's life, by their attitudes toward strong drink. Ames wins the contest.

From an editor's point of view, these are really questions of biography. One is speculating about Dreiser's motives and intentions, and about Arthur Henry's and the publisher's as well. One is constructing roles for people to play—Dreiser as realistic and blunt, though willing to compromise in order to get his novel into print; Henry as facile and shallow, interested primarily in moving Dreiser's narrative along more quickly; Doubleday, Page and Co. as keen to remove anything from the text that might cause trouble with reviewers and public moralists. The evidence here is no weaker or stronger than that used by most biographers. Textual editors are biographers too, though they sometimes cloak their speculations and imaginative flights in technical-sounding terminology.

One can raise questions about drinking in *Sister Carrie* (or about similar conundrums in the text) not only in published essays such as this one, but in classrooms as well. In this case, students might be encouraged to think of *Sister Carrie* as a gambling machine. Pull the lever and only one reference to alcohol appears—but which one? Pull it again, and two references appear—but which two? Pull it once more and all three appear. How does the interpretation change after each pull? This would not simply be a literary game. An editor could justify any combination, so long as the references to Hurstwood's drinking remained in the text—and it might be instructive to speculate about the effect on the novel if those references were cut as well.

I hope that teachers and other interpreters of *Sister Carrie* will engage in this kind of exercise and will use the textual apparatus in the Pennsylvania text to ferret out other points at which a restoration changes one's reading of the novel, in a small or large way. That's what textual editors are supposed to do—stir up the silt at the bottom of the pool. Editors shouldn't claim that the text they present is calm, shimmering, and serenely perfect. They should instead muddy things up and stimulate discussion, as I've tried to do here.

NOTES

1. See the Pennsylvania *Sister Carrie,* 525, and West, *A "Sister Carrie" Portfolio,* 64–65.

2. In a similar scene in *Jennie Gerhardt,* a reference to drinking by Lester Kane was removed. Between manuscript and print, in fact, nearly all mention of alcohol was cut from the text. In the passage in question, Lester has learned from a distraught Jennie that she has a child—little Vesta, whose existence she has been concealing. Vesta's caretaker has come to the apartment that Jennie and Lester are sharing and has told Jennie that Vesta is dangerously ill. Jennie rushes away to minister to the child, but not before Lester has extracted from her the information that she has a daughter. While Jennie is away, Lester meditates (rather uncharitably) on Jennie's past history. Almost his first action is to leave the apartment and stop "at the first convenient saloon" for alcohol (Pennsylvania edition, 208). Thus when he confronts Jennie later, after she returns, he is feeling the effects of the alcohol. Although his demeanor toward her is angry at first, he is quickly disarmed by the simplicity and honesty of her explanations. This reference to Lester's drinking, however, was cut between manuscript and the 1911 Harper first edition. Since the ribbon typescript on which the Harper editors worked does not survive, one cannot know whether they or Dreiser removed the reference, but other mentions of drinking (by Old Gerhardt, for example, on p. 271 of the Pennsylvania edition) were also removed before the Harper text was published. I restored Lester's visit to the saloon to the Pennsylvania *Jennie Gerhardt.*

## DOUBLE QUOTES AND DOUBLE
## MEANINGS IN *JENNIE GERHARDT*

Dreiser's 1911 novel *Jennie Gerhardt* is structured around a series of deathbed scenes. There is the death of Jennie's mother; of Old Gerhardt, her father; of Vesta, her daughter; and finally of Lester Kane, her former lover. In each scene Jennie is deprived of a person dear to her, though in some of the scenes there are confessions by the dying person to help Jennie bear the loss. The most important of these scenes is the final one—Lester's death in a hotel room in Chicago. Letty Gerald, Lester's wife, is away in Europe. Lester therefore asks that Jennie be brought to him. In the years since he ended his arrangement with her, agreeing to support her but not see her, she has been living on the South Side of Chicago, using the name "Mrs. J. G. Stover" and raising two orphan children. Jennie is contacted by Lester's lawyer, who takes her to Lester's hotel. She comes to his room, and they exchange small talk. Then the scene builds in intensity. Lester apologizes to Jennie: "I haven't been satisfied with the way we parted," he tells her. "It wasn't the right thing, after all. I haven't been any happier. I'm sorry. I wish now, for my own peace of mind, that I hadn't done it."[1] A few lines later one comes upon the emotional high point of the novel—Lester's final and long-delayed declaration of love for Jennie. The passage is reproduced below exactly as it appears in the Harper and Brothers 1911 first-edition text:

> "Well, I've told you now, and I feel better. You're a good woman, Jennie, and you're kind to come to me this way." I loved you. I love you now. I want to tell you that. It seems strange, but you're the only woman I ever did love truly. We should never have parted.
>
> Jennie caught her breath. It was the one thing she had waited for all these years—this testimony. It was the one thing that could make everything right—this confession of spiritual if not material union. Now

she could live happily. Now die so. "Oh, Lester," she exclaimed with a sob, and pressed his hand. He returned the pressure. There was a little silence. Then he spoke again.

"How are the two orphans?" he asked. (422–23)

The careful reader will have noticed that, in the Harper text, the double quotation marks follow the word *way.* All that comes after—Lester's moving confession of love and regret—is outside the quotation marks. Strictly speaking, he does not utter these words.

One does not wish to make more of a single punctuation mark than is reasonable. Probably this is only a tiny soiled fish swimming about in this particular textual ocean. But the error, if error it is, comes at a pivotal point in the narrative. Does Lester really tell Jennie that he loves her, or is his speech something she imagines, something uttered by a voice within her own mind, a voice telling her what she wants to hear? One hopes that this is not the case, that Dreiser has not undercut an emotionally important moment near the end of this book by the kind of irony that only a proofreader might notice. But hoping is not enough: the surviving evidence must be examined and the history of the passage reconstructed if the proper punctuation of the passage is to be known.

Dreiser began composing *Jennie Gerhardt* on 6 January 1901 and made a strong start over the next few months, producing over forty chapters before deciding that he had made an error in his depiction of Jennie's character. He put aside all he had written after chapter 15 and rewrote from that point on to a new chapter 30. He had a typescript prepared of these thirty chapters, revised that typescript, and had a clean typescript made, probably to show to publishers. These two partial typescripts, and the holograph drafts that precede them, survive today in the Theodore Dreiser Papers at the University of Pennsylvania.

In 1902 Dreiser began to suffer from neurasthenia, or nerve sickness. He signed a contract for *Jennie Gerhardt* with the J. F. Taylor Company, a small New York publishing and remainder house, and Taylor provided advances to Dreiser in 1902–3 totaling some $750. Dreiser, however, was unable to push his manuscript ahead—indeed, was unable to do sustained literary work of any kind. He eventually recovered from his nervous troubles and reentered the world of journalism early in 1904. He rose to the position of editor in chief of Butterick Publications, a firm that issued several women's magazines, but his duties there prevented him from returning to his novel.

# JENNIE GERHARDT

through. He couldn't stand many more paroxysms like the last one.

"I couldn't go, Jennie, without seeing you again," he observed, when the slight twinge ceased and he was free to think again. "I've always wanted to say to you, Jennie," he went on, "that I haven't been satisfied with the way we parted. It wasn't the right thing, after all. I haven't been any happier. I'm sorry. I wish now, for my own peace of mind, that I hadn't done it."

"Don't say that, Lester," she demurred, going over in her mind all that had been between them. This was such a testimony to their real union—their real spiritual compatibility. "It's all right. It doesn't make any difference. You've been very good to me. I wouldn't have been satisfied to have you lose your fortune. It couldn't be that way. I've been a lot better satisfied as it is. It's been hard, but, dear, everything is hard at times." She paused.

"No," he said. "It wasn't right. The thing wasn't worked out right from the start; but that wasn't your fault. I'm sorry. I wanted to tell you that. I'm glad I'm here to do it."

"Don't talk that way, Lester—please don't," she pleaded. "It's all right. You needn't be sorry. There's nothing to be sorry for. You have always been so good to me. Why, when I think—" she stopped, for it was hard for her to speak. She was choking with affection and sympathy. She pressed his hands. She was recalling the house he took for her family in Cleveland, his generous treatment of Gerhardt, all the long ago tokens of love and kindness.

"Well, I've told you now, and I feel better. You're a good woman, Jennie, and you're kind to come to me this way." I loved you. I love you now. I want to tell you that. It seems strange, but you're the only woman I ever did love truly. We should never have parted.

Jennie caught her breath. It was the one thing she

422

49

It was not until 1910, after he had resigned from Butterick, that Dreiser resumed serious labor on *Jennie Gerhardt*. He finished a draft during the last months of 1910, had this version completely retyped, in ribbon and carbon copies, and showed it to several friends whose literary judgment he trusted. Partly because of their suggestions, and partly because of his own second thoughts, he rewrote the ending of the novel. In the first complete version of *Jennie Gerhardt*, Lester defied his respectable family, ignored his material interests, and married Jennie. In the new conclusion, Lester knuckles under to his family, severs his relationship with Jennie, and eventually marries Letty Gerald, a woman of wealth, setting up the deathbed scene in the hotel room.

In composing this new conclusion, Dreiser inscribed fresh holograph drafts of the final chapters of the book, had these new chapters typed in ribbon and carbon copies, and grafted the new sections onto the earlier typed chapters. The ribbon copy of this composite typescript went to Harper and Brothers; the carbon went to England for consideration by British publishers. This carbon came back to Dreiser, was sent to H. L. Mencken for an opinion, and was again returned to Dreiser. Its travels thereafter are obscure, but it eventually came to rest in the Albert and Shirley Small Special Collections Library, University of Virginia. It is an important document for our purposes here, since it is now the only complete prepublication typescript of *Jennie Gerhardt* extant.

The ribbon copy was revised and cut by the Harper editor Ripley Hitchcock and his assistants. So extensive were their alterations that a fresh typescript had to be prepared for the compositor of the first edition. Hitchcock returned a portion of the revised and cut ribbon copy to Dreiser on 1 June 1911, but no part of this ribbon copy is known to survive.[2] The fresh typescript prepared by Harper and used by the compositor has also not survived, and no galleys or page proofs are extant.

A simple hypothesis will explain the misplaced quotation marks. Dreiser added Lester's declaration of love, and Jennie's reaction, in a lost stage of revision. Either he or a typist or compositor forgot to move the quotation marks to include the new words. The documents that survive support this hypothesis. In the extant holograph draft of the passage, Lester avoids the subject of love. He apologizes to Jennie for mishandling their relationship but says nothing more. At the point of the crux, the manuscript reads as follows:

> "Well, I've told you now and I feel better. Your a good woman and your kind to come this way."

She could see that sickness had taken away some of the natural phlegmatic sternness of his character.

"How are the two orphans?" he added.

This passage does not appear in either of the typescripts at Penn; they extend only through chapter 30, and Lester's death occurs in chapter 61. The passage does appear, however, in the Barrett typescript at Virginia. There it is virtually identical to the manuscript text. Lester still apologizes to Jennie but makes no declaration of love; there is no outpouring of gratitude from her.

The expansion of Lester's speech, and the addition of Jennie's reaction to his words, must therefore have been executed by Dreiser either on the original ribbon copy of the typescript, or on the Harper typescript, or in galleys, or in page proof. Although none of these survive, one can reconstruct what probably happened. Dreiser added the new lines in a margin, or perhaps (given the length of the addition) on a separate leaf of paper. He must have written a note, drawn an arrow, or put in a caret to indicate where the new passage should go, but he apparently neglected to delete the quotation marks after *way* and to add new ones after *parted*. The typist or compositor simply followed directions, and no one caught the error in a subsequent proofreading.

Is there a chance that the passage was added by someone other than Dreiser—perhaps by an editor at Harper who wanted Lester finally to overcome his scruples and declare his love for Jennie? That is certainly possible. A full collation of the Barrett typescript with the first edition demonstrates that the Harper editors freely altered and augmented Dreiser's text. The changes made at Harper fall into several categories. Some mute sexual frankness; others remove references to alcohol; still others blunt Dreiser's criticisms of organized religion. Of particular interest was the tendency of Hitchcock's subeditors to descend on key spots of the story and milk them for emotion and sentiment. In the text that he had originally submitted, Dreiser's method was to keep the narrative flat at such moments; he avoided words or phrasing that would elicit an emotional reaction from the reader, preferring to let the facts of the story speak. The Harper editors rewrote these spots and added words and phrasings that are meant to call forth emotion and sentiment. One's suspicions are aroused: was Lester's deathbed speech introduced at the Harper offices in an attempt to make the scene more touching?

Perhaps, but stylistic evidence suggests that Dreiser added the passage. The paragraph containing Jennie's reaction—from "Jennie caught her breath" to "Then he spoke again"—is written in his characteristic prose. The dashes, the halting diction, the wording of "this confession of spiritual if not material union," the phrase "a little silence"—all are of a piece with Dreiser's style during this period. One's impulse is to believe that these words are Dreiser's and, by extension, that Lester's confession of love was written by Dreiser as well.

Judgments about style, though, are not as strong as decisions based on documentary evidence. It is therefore good to report that a 13 March 1911 letter to Dreiser from his friend Charles B. De Camp, preserved in the Penn archive, gives added weight to the speculation that Dreiser added Lester's deathbed speech. The biographical facts are important here. As I have said, Dreiser finished an initial version of *Jennie Gerhardt* in January 1911 and had it typed in two copies, a ribbon and a carbon. These he showed to various friends and associates, asking for a reaction from each one. The best-known reactions are those of the critic James Huneker, who praised the story but criticized Dreiser's "opaque" style, and of Freemont Rider, who advised Dreiser not to let Lester and Jennie marry—advice Dreiser took in revising the last chapters of his novel.[3] De Camp was also among these early readers. He had been one of Dreiser's assistants when Dreiser was an editor at the publisher Street and Smith in 1904–5; Dreiser remembered him years later as "so wise, so sensitive, so esthetic and kind."[4] De Camp showed some promise as a writer but had a weakness for alcohol and died of pneumonia at a relatively young age.

Like Huneker and Rider, De Camp had a mixed opinion of *Jennie Gerhardt.* Below is the text of his letter to Dreiser:

March 13th, 1911

Dear Theodore,

I sent the MS to Adachi today.[5]

Your novel is a tremendously big and impressive thing—solid hewed out of life. I don't know of any one who has so depicted American life in the broad terms of human nature, with so much objective sincerity and absence of prejudice. It is a great achievement and I congratulate you from my heart.

You have asked me to criticise it and I am going to try to do so, briefly, for I want a chance to talk it over with you.

It is too life-like. By that I mean that it is inconsequential and not sufficiently inevitable. You feel that it might have eventuated any of several ways without making much difference. It contains dramative motives and potentialities which never develop, as in the coming of Gerhardt to the

Hyde Park home, with his belief in Jennie's marriage—and in the visit of O'Brien to Jennie at a critical moment & its lack of any effect on Lester's action in separating from her. However these instances are not important. It is the lack of significance in the story as a whole that I mean.

I know what you mean the story to show (as much as you want to show anything). You state it in your afterword—a most beautiful bit of prose. But I do not think that is enough—otherwise any series of misfortunes or blows from the "system" we call life would suffice. Perhaps the lack that I feel comes from something in your own temperament & attitude: that any true picture of life doesn't show anything one way or the other. Of course, you know I am not talking about a "lesson" or a "moral" & yet in a larger sense I think art has to draw one, implicitly at least. If life is merely thrown down in front of you, as it were, in a heap it is depressing. And if any one thing will limit the wide success of this book it will be that depressing effect.

Now I think this effect springs specifically from the absence of any *uplifting* spiritual reaction on the part of any of the characters. Perhaps you mean it to in Jennie and in a way, yes. But Jennie to me is too passive a creature to show anything satisfying. I don't doubt she represents something terribly moving and appealing to you. But I think she is too pitiful to furnish much real tragic interest. Lester, on the other hand, interested me tremendously, and it is right here in finishing with him that I think a slight change would help a lot. You have him very naturally say but few words to Jennie on his death-bed but I think you could make him just as naturally say a little more. He is introduced to the reader as a strong, self-confident person with very materialistic ideas of life & certainly no spiritual views on marriage. Now whether he loves Jennie very intensely or not he has undoubtedly come to feel that there is a peculiar & spiritual relationship between them. I would have him confess it at the last—that theirs was a true marriage (or at least his truest marriage) and that there is a spiritual something in life that he was ignorant of. (I am not talking about the sanctity of marriage.) That would be *his* spiritual reaction & give significance to his experience with life. Think that over. I haven't been able to think of any other generally different ending.

But one thing more: I would cut out the funeral & depot scenes. It intensifies the woe rather gratuitously, I think—I was going to say

cheaply. I would have her say goodbye to his body in the bed & leave—
but of this part more when I see you.

Ever Sincerely,

C. B. De Camp[6]

When De Camp criticizes *Jennie Gerhardt* as "too life-like," he means that
Dreiser does not sufficiently differentiate one scene from another in his narrative. This was probably a conscious attempt at realism on Dreiser's part, but
De Camp seems to find it frustrating. He is asking Dreiser to introduce some
directions or hints for the reader. Which moments in the story are meant to
be crucial? Which of the plot shifts will eventually be important? De Camp
does perceive that the central dialectic in the novel is between Lester's "mate-
rialism" and Jennie's "spiritualism." Lester is a pessimistic determinist; Jennie
is emotional and intuitive, relying more on instinct than on intellect. She
is psychologically whole and capable of love; Lester is crippled by his pessi-
mism and is probably unable to feel love, at least as Jennie feels it. De Camp
wants Dreiser to resolve this dialectic by having Lester admit to Jennie on his
deathbed that "there is a spiritual something in life that he was ignorant of."
Ultimately Dreiser did not give a set philosophical speech to Lester. It appears,
however, that he was persuaded by De Camp to have Lester tell Jennie that he
loves her.

Surviving copies of De Camp's letter help confirm that it was Dreiser who
added Lester's speech to the text. Dreiser had De Camp's handwritten letter transcribed by a typist in order to show the comments to other readers
of *Jennie Gerhardt*. (Apparently the reading and assessment of the novel was
something of a collective enterprise.) At the top of De Camp's original letter,
someone other than Dreiser has written "6 more copies of this." Dreiser kept
one of the six copies for himself; it survives today in his papers, along with
De Camp's handwritten original. At the top of the original letter, Dreiser has
written "*Jennie Gerhardt*" in black pen. Then, in this identical black pen, he
has marked parentheses around the sentences in the typed transcription which
urge that Lester "say a little more" to Jennie. These are the ten sentences, in
the sixth paragraph of the letter, from "But Jennie" to "experience with life."
One assumes that this is the portion of the letter Dreiser found most useful,
the advice from De Camp that he decided to follow. He did not follow all of
De Camp's suggestions: we can be thankful, for example, that he did not cut
Lester's funeral or the final scene at the train station—scenes that are among

the best in the novel. But it would appear that he did add Lester's deathbed declaration of love.

What of the subsequent textual history of this deathbed speech, with its misplaced mark of punctuation? Was the error ever corrected? A check of subsequent impressions from the plates of the Harper 1911 edition shows that no change was ever made. In reprintings issued by Harper, A. L. Burt, Boni and Liveright, Doubleday, Simon and Schuster, and World, the quotation marks invariably follow *way.* The British edition, published by Constable in 1928, repeats the error, and the mistake is still present in the photo-offset replating of this edition issued by Schocken Books in 1982. Only the Dell paperback edition, published in November 1963, corrects the error. There the quotation marks are moved to include Lester's entire speech.

The most important thing about this crux is not the decision that faces an editor of a scholarly edition of *Jennie Gerhardt.* Given the stylistic evidence plus De Camp's letter as marked by Dreiser, the likelihood is strong that it was Dreiser who added Lester's confession of love and Jennie's reaction to it. This happened in a late stage of revision, and no one properly repunctuated the passage. Dreiser probably did not have the reading corrected in 1928 because it was never called to his attention. Perhaps no one ever noticed the mistake. It is quite easy to miss when reading the passage because one is so thoroughly caught up in the drama and emotion of the scene. It would be more reassuring if other documentary evidence were extant, particularly if the stage of the text in which Dreiser added the passage had survived. The evidence does indicate, however, that this is nothing more than a typographical error and that it should be corrected. Lester does utter his heartfelt words to Jennie; they are not a product of her imagination. Following this line of reasoning, I retained the added words in the Pennsylvania text of *Jennie Gerhardt* and moved the quotation marks to the proper spot. I also included the original text, without Lester's confession, in an appendix.

Dreiser did not add this important passage until late in the compositional process, and then only at the urging of someone else. What would *Jennie Gerhardt* have been like had he not added the passage? Here one's interpretive faculties come into play. In the manuscript and in the Barrett typescript, the effect of Lester's deathbed scene is different from its effect in the first edition. In the manuscript and typescript, Lester and Jennie smile and make inconsequential talk; then he offers her a straightforward apology for his behavior during their earlier relationship. The scene appears to be building to an emotional climax, but Lester does not seem to know what to say. He temporizes, the moment passes, and talk returns to the two orphans under Jennie's care. Her voice soothes him, and he persuades her not to leave. She stays nearby in the hotel until he dies.

Yet is such a flat scene not more typical of Dreiser's writing than the powerful but sentimental scene created by Lester's declaration of love? Great moments do come in life, moments in which past and present seem briefly to coalesce, but often the participants in these small dramas do not recognize the significance of these moments and they pass. According to one's viewpoint, then, the unrevised scene might be considered more Dreiserian, more appropriate for this naturalistic novel, more nearly in line with the rest of its philosophical argument, than the revised scene.

*Jennie Gerhardt* is in part about such scenes as these, about their validity in a system of human conduct. Dreiser seems to be exploring the meaning of such scenes. At several points in the novel, his characters apologize for past behavior and make gestures toward reconciliation. Jennie, for example, attempts to apologize to her father in chapter 14 for having had a child out of wedlock. Old Gerhardt grudgingly forgives her but pushes her away when she tries to be affectionate. "It had been a frigid meeting," comments the narrator (117). Jennie is kind and generous to her father during the years that follow, and one senses that his opinion of her changes, but he never tells her that he forgives her. Indeed, Old Gerhardt does not come to any reconciliation with Jennie until he is literally at the point of death. His dying words are "You've been good to me. You're a good woman" (346). With this she must be satisfied; it is all she will ever have from him.

In chapter 60, the chapter immediately preceding the one in which Lester makes his deathbed confession to Jennie, there is another such scene of partial reconciliation. Lester's brother Robert, from whom Lester has been estranged for some years over the matter of Jennie, asks that Lester meet him in Chicago. The ostensible purpose of the meeting is to discuss a business deal involving the Western Crucible Steel Company, a firm in which both Robert and Lester are major shareholders. Robert proposes that Lester acquire a block of stock which has lately come up for sale; then, if Lester will pool his voting power with Robert's, they can get rid of the firm's manager and take control of the business. It is an attractive proposition financially, but Lester realizes that Robert's real purpose is to effect a reconciliation. "This was the olive branch," thinks Lester, "the control of a property worth in the neighborhood of a million and a half" (410). It is typical of Robert, whose business ethics are less gentlemanly and humane than Lester's, to make the gesture in this way. To his credit, Lester sees Robert's offer for what it is. "I don't want it," says Lester. "I'm rich enough anyhow" (411). Lester also rejects Robert's proposal for a full reconciliation. "Bygones are bygones," Lester says. "I'm perfectly willing to talk with you from time to time. That's all you want. This other thing is simply a sop with which to plaster an old wound" (411). Lester's forthright behavior should be applauded. Conciliatory gestures, made years after the fact, are easy and inexpensive. Robert has had things his way; Lester and Jennie have suffered. Now Robert wants his past behavior to be forgiven, but Lester denies him the satisfaction, probably because he doubts Robert's sincerity.

By the same token, one must question the sincerity of Lester's dying declaration of love to Jennie. It is too easy for him to say these words. He has suffered, to be sure, but not nearly as deeply as she has. After he shed Jennie and married Letty Gerald, his society friends, in another variation of the pattern, quickly forgave him and welcomed him back into their circle. Past misdeeds were forgotten. He and Letty lived an easy, indolent existence, and he did not have to pay very heavily for his past offenses. Jennie, by contrast, will pay for the rest of her life.

Is it not more in character for Lester *not* to tell Jennie, on his deathbed, that he loves her? Surely he must know that such a confession will cost him little, that it is fundamentally an insincere thing to do. There is nothing he can say to her now that will make up for the years of embarrassment and shame he has brought her. Perhaps Lester recognizes this; perhaps it is why, in the original, unrevised text, he does not tell Jennie that he loves her. In the revised text, though, he makes the gesture, and Jennie, to her credit, responds generously: "It was the one thing she had waited for all these years—this testimony. It was the one thing that could make everything right—this confession of spiritual if not material union. Now she could live happily. Now die so" (422–23). Perhaps Jennie too is caught up in the emotion of the moment. Perhaps later she will see that Lester's words were easy ones to utter. Deathbed declarations are cheap because one does not have to follow up on them.

Thus far I have argued in such a way as to cast doubt on the wisdom of Dreiser's decision to add Lester's declaration of love and Jennie's reaction to it. But one can shift to another interpretation, one which argues for Dreiser's additions as improvements, as parts of an overall design for the novel which he fulfilled only with this late revision. It could be that Dreiser wanted us, in this penultimate chapter of the book, to contrast Jennie with Lester. Perhaps we are meant to see Jennie's generous and selfless outpouring of gratitude, her ready acceptance of Lester's apology, against the scene between Robert and Lester in the previous chapter. Throughout this novel Jennie's instinctive approach to life, her sensitivity to beauty, and her awareness of the underlying pattern of nature are presented as alternatives to Lester's bleak mechanistic determinism. Lester's response to Robert's proposal is consistent with his skepticism and inertia; Jennie's response to Lester's confession of love is consistent with her largeness of spirit.

Such an interpretation is attractive, but the reasoning might be flawed. The pattern I have just sketched might be wholly adventitious—an accidental product of an impulsive last-minute addition by Dreiser, the consequences of which he did not fully foresee. My reasoning might fall into circularity: I discern a pattern in the text; therefore Dreiser must have meant to create this pattern; therefore any revisions he made which help to perpetuate this pattern must be honored.

An editor must be careful in deploying a critical interpretation to support a decision to emend. Interpretations can cut both ways. It is probably best to fall back on the evidence that survives. Lester's confession and Jennie's reaction were added in a late stage of revision. They were likely added by Dreiser, responding to De Camp's suggestions. The wording and style of the added sentences suggest that they were written by Dreiser. It is plausible to assume that Dreiser, or a typist or compositor, forgot to move the quotation marks to include Lester's new words. And it is unlikely that Dreiser meant to hang significant meaning on the positioning of a single set of quotation marks. He was not that type of writer; one does not find that kind of thing in his other books. He never corrected the error because no one brought it to his attention.

This single misplaced mark of punctuation provides a point in the text from which to open up its compositional history and its critical interpretation. We see Dreiser at work on a crucial scene and are prompted to examine the implications of that scene more closely than we otherwise might. We come to understand the published form of the scene more fully by contrasting it with an earlier, less satisfying, but perhaps more realistic version of it. We also see the many varieties of evidence—biographical, documentary, critical, and stylistic—on which a textual decision of this kind can hinge.

NOTES

1. Theodore Dreiser, *Jennie Gerhardt* (New York: Harper, 1911), 422. Subsequent quotations, cited parenthetically, are from this edition or, when indicated, from the Pennsylvania edition of 1992.
2. Hitchcock to Dreiser, 1 June 1911, Dreiser Papers, University of Pennsylvania.

3.   See Huneker to Dreiser, 4 June 1911, Dreiser Papers; also Dreiser's responses to both Huneker and Rider in *Letters of Theodore Dreiser: A Selection*, 3 vols., ed. Robert H. Elias (Philadelphia: University of Pennsylvania Press, 1959), 1:110, 117.

4.   Dreiser to Mencken, 8 March 1943, in *Dreiser-Mencken Letters*, 684.

5.   Adachi Kinnosuke was a journalist whose articles on Japanese culture and other Far East topics were appearing in *Harper's*, the *Century*, *Collier's*, and Dreiser's *Delineator*. His appreciative letter to Dreiser, written after reading *Jennie Gerhardt* in typescript, is in the Dreiser Collection. Adachi was the author of *Iroka: Tales of Japan* (1900) and *Manchuria: A Survey* (1925). He was one of Dreiser's supporters during the controversy over the suppression of *The "Genius"* several years later.

6.   Dreiser Papers.

# EDITING PRIVATE PAPERS

*Three Examples from Dreiser*

When scholarly editors discuss theory and procedure, they usually focus on public texts—poems, stories, novels, essays, and drama scripts prepared by authors for print or performance. Editors less frequently give consideration to private papers: letters, journals, diaries, fragments, trial drafts, and aborted manuscripts. Questions of presentation and audience are foremost with private papers; annotation and intention also figure into the mix. Emendation is not usually a large issue: because the documents almost always survive in single copies, there is no opportunity to create a text from multiple versions. Questions of emendation are usually straightforward, involving only obvious or demonstrable errors.

Problems, however, do arise with the editing of private texts. In this essay I will discuss several that presented themselves during the editing of some important documents that survive in the papers of Theodore Dreiser at the University of Pennsylvania. The editions in question, all published by the University of Pennsylvania Press, are Dreiser's *American Diaries* (1982), *An Amateur Laborer* (1983), and *Russian Diary* (1996).[1] These are private texts. Either Dreiser did not write them for publication, or he set out to create them for print but at some point abandoned the effort. The decisions discussed here were difficult to make. Some of them worked out well and others less well, though it is hard now to see how the choices might have been made differently.

The first set of decisions had to do with seven diaries that Dreiser kept during the first three decades of the twentieth century. These diaries were brought together and published in 1982 under the title *American Diaries, 1902–1926*. All seven diaries were kept by Dreiser while he was living in the United States, though in different locations: Philadelphia, Savannah, Greenwich Village, Indiana, the Jersey Shore, Hollywood, and Florida. Dreiser was an intermittent diarist, keeping journals in periods of unhappiness or travel or intense creativity. He saved the diaries; they are important sources of information for anyone interested in his life and writing.

Dreiser was not a confessional or meditative diarist. In most entries the style is workmanlike and the text often no more than a record of the day's activities. Some passages are memorable, however, and the accumulation of detail (as in his novels) is arresting and revealing. One learns how Dreiser lived, what he did, whom he saw, what women he was involved with, what he was writing, how he was pushing ahead in his literary career. And in one of them, the 1902–3 Philadelphia diary, he left a harrowing record of a period of neurasthenia that was pivotal in his life.

The first question was whether to correct the texts at all. Dreiser was a poor speller and grammarian. He knew this and employed personal editors and amanuenses to help put his public writings into shape. The seven diaries, however, were private writings, not meant for publication. The prevailing orthodoxy is that such texts should be put into print with as little emendation as possible in an effort to capture something of the flavor of the originals. The problem was that Dreiser had suffered during his career from a perception among critics that he was badly educated, clumsy and even oafish in literary style—that he possessed a rude, natural talent for writing and, almost by accident, had managed to write three or four of the most powerful novels of his time. Would an edition of the diaries, preserving all of Dreiser's faults in grammar, spelling, and style, reinforce this image? Would it give ammunition to those critics (still very much in operation) who want to dismiss Dreiser's work as subliterate?

There was the example of F. Scott Fitzgerald's letters to contemplate. Fitzgerald, a Midwesterner like Dreiser, was an extremely erratic speller, and his grammar, like Dreiser's, was not always up to par. But Fitzgerald wrote wonderful letters—funny, revealing, newsy, and full of fine turns of phrase and perceptive insights. In 1963 Andrew Turnbull, the author of a nonacademic biography of Fitzgerald, edited *The Letters of F. Scott Fitzgerald,* a lengthy collection published by Charles Scribner's Sons. Turnbull and Scribner's made the decision to clean up the texts, silently correcting Fitzgerald's misspellings and remedying his grammatical lapses. Fitzgerald, like Dreiser, had drawn criticism during his career for being undereducated and intellectually lightweight. His shortcomings in orthography and grammar seemed of a piece with that portrait. Turnbull and Scribner's did not say so—there is no word in the edition about the editing of the texts—but apparently they decided to short-circuit such criticisms by repairing Fitzgerald's mistakes for him. Would it be advisable to do the same for Dreiser?

The decision for the *American Diaries* was not to correct the texts. To do so would alter the diaries in a fundamental way; they were therefore presented in a near-diplomatic transcription. Such misspellings as "recieve," "excitment," "opourtunity," "your" (for "you're"), and "accross" were preserved, as were faulty agreements between subjects and verbs, misplaced or dangling modifiers, floating participles, and errant pronoun references. Underlinings were printed as underscores rather than italics; odd spacing was reproduced as nearly as was possible in a printed medium. Some emendation was necessary: a few substantive changes were made to clarify confusing or nonsensical language, and periods were added where necessary, because Dreiser, in his haste, often omitted them from the ends of sentences. Place-names were corrected when possible, and erroneous dates for the entries were repaired. To have left dates and place-names uncorrected would have preserved nothing essential and would have confused scholars and biographers. Emendations of these kinds were recorded in an apparatus.

Perhaps the most interesting of the seven diaries was kept by Dreiser in 1917 and 1918 while he was living the bohemian life in Greenwich Village. He was involved during this period with a woman named Estelle Bloom Kubitz, whom he calls "Bert" or sometimes "Gloom" in the diary. She functioned as his secretary and typist and was his lover as well. But Dreiser, who was unapologetic about his sexual varietism, was involved with other women during this period. Estelle was unhappy about the situation, though she had the same privileges. As his secretary she had access to his papers; and at some point, perhaps while he was away from the city, she made a typed transcription of this diary. It contains the names of Dreiser's lovers and details of his various sexual liaisons, along with much else. Estelle later turned this transcription over to H. L. Mencken, Dreiser's ally in the literary press, who was himself involved with her sister Marion. We know from Mencken's own letters and private diaries that he was curious about Dreiser's sexual escapades; probably Estelle was aware of this and thought that the transcript would entertain him. Mencken also functioned as a confidant for her, and she had confessed to him her frustration over Dreiser's womanizing. Perhaps she thought that the diary transcript would be documentary proof of her complaints about Dreiser's wanderings. Whatever the case, Mencken saved the transcript and left it among the papers that he bequeathed to the New York Public Library— a happy circumstance, because the original diary is not known to survive. Estelle Kubitz's transcription is all that we have.

From an editor's standpoint, this transcription presents some problems. Estelle was in the habit of correcting Dreiser's spelling and grammar as she typed his essays and stories and novel chapters. She performed the same services as she was transcribing this diary. Thus the surviving text of the Greenwich Village diary is more nearly correct and finished than the texts of the other diaries. Should characteristic Dreiser misspellings and other blunders be editorially reintroduced into the text of this particular diary to create an impression of authenticity? Surely not: this would involve much editorial intervention and be highly artificial. The result, however, is peculiar. The Greenwich Village diary, falling third in the published volume, presents readers with a text that is suddenly correct and polished, unlike the ones before and after it. Only if these readers have read the textual introduction will they understand what is happening.

The published edition of the *American Diaries* was widely reviewed and discussed. A voice not available before—Dreiser's voice in the diaries, which is quite unlike his fictional voice—was now heard. The diaries generated discussion of Dreiser and his career and were of great use to Richard Lingeman, whose two-volume biography of Dreiser has become standard.[2] The edition was a success: the printed entries do capture most of the flavor of the originals without seeming fussy or contrived.

The second of the Dreiser documents that needed editing was a manuscript entitled "An Amateur Laborer." This manuscript, produced in 1904, is related closely to the Philadelphia diary mentioned above, the journal in which he kept a record of his neurasthenia. By 1904 Dreiser had recovered sufficiently well to think of putting these experiences into a nonfiction account and publishing it. He began the manuscript, describing first his nerve sickness, then tracing his mental decline and detailing his musings on suicide. He told of being rescued by his songwriter brother Paul and recounted his activities at William Muldoon's sanitarium, a rehabilitation camp to which Paul sent him. Finally Dreiser told about some of his subsequent experiences as a day laborer on the New York Central Railroad. A doctor had prescribed outdoor labor to Dreiser as a cure for his depression, but he found himself inept and clumsy as a physical worker. Hence his title "An Amateur Laborer."

Dreiser never finished this book or published it in its entirety. He could not interest a publisher in the account; he produced twenty-five chapters in more or less finished form and left at least as much other fragmentary material with the manuscript—trial drafts of episodes that were meant for later chapters or sometimes only passages or sentences that he thought might be worked into the narrative. Dreiser drew on this material repeatedly during his later career. Some of it was used in his novel *The "Genius"* (1915) and some in newspaper and magazine articles. Other laboring experiences found their way into the sketches in *Twelve Men* (1919) or into short stories. These later reworkings depart considerably from the narratives that Dreiser had set down in the original "Laborer" manuscript. The unpublished manuscript, written soon after the experiences on which it was based, was almost surely the most reliable of the accounts.

This manuscript reveals a good deal about how Dreiser assembled a book, during this period at least. The surviving materials suggest that he would first compose in fragments and short bursts, setting down incidents or remembered emotions in brief sections of holograph. These he stitched together into a narrative, providing a thematic or moral framework and making a fair copy as he went along. The twenty-five completed chapters are in relatively finished form, verbally and structurally. They appear to be fair copies, ready for a typist. The fragments, on the other hand, are the leading edge of the project—disordered and preliminary, as if Dreiser had yet to decide how they might fit into the narrative.

How could a printed edition reflect these characteristics? What distinctions could be made between finished and unfinished material? The decision was to present the twenty-five completed chapters as public texts, with spelling corrected and grammatical faults remedied. This did not demand heavy emendation, but it did require some correcting, and the texts lost something. They were certainly not rendered in such a way as to capture their original flavor. An argument to print them in diplomatic transcription would have carried a good deal of force. Whenever unfinished work is primped up for publication, it invites reviewers to consider it as fully realized writing. This was clearly not the case with the first twenty-five chapters of "An Amateur Laborer." No one knows what Dreiser would have done to these chapters had he completed the entire narrative, but he would surely have worked further on them. Still, he had brought these units to a finished enough form to warrant our publication of them as public texts. After all, the converse is also true: if interesting but not fully completed material is published in diplomatic transcription, it is sometimes considered to be only of passing interest and is ignored.

The fragments, however, were clearly private texts. A selection of these was made and included in the rear of the volume, but with misspellings and grammar faults and incomplete punctuation and other peculiarities preserved.

This strategy revealed their contrasting character, reflected Dreiser's composing methods, and prevented the fragments from being read as fully finished
work. The only disappointment was that it was impossible to include all of
them. Many of them repeated one another; in a few cases, two versions of the
same incident were included in the published edition for comparison, but in
most cases only the fullest and latest draft of a passage was used. Other material was so fragmentary or brief as not to have much meaning when read alone.
Thus the final volume, *An Amateur Laborer,* published in 1983, was an editorial
confection. It presented a work in progress, showing the nearly finished chapters as public texts and the parts still under composition as private texts. The
resulting book, though artificially constructed, was a successful piece of editorial work. It did a good job of reflecting the state of the surviving document.

The third of the documents, a diary kept by Dreiser during a trip to Soviet
Russia in 1927 and 1928, was the most difficult to edit. Dreiser was invited
by the Soviet government in October 1927 to come to Moscow for a cel-
ebration of the tenth anniversary of the revolution. He was one among some
fifteen hundred international celebrities—writers, artists, journalists, political
figures, and others—who were so summoned. The Soviets hoped that good
impressions of their experiment in government would be carried away and
that the writers, in particular, would publish favorable accounts of what they
had seen. The hosts managed the tours carefully, showing only the most successful factories and farming collectives and allowing the visitors to interview
only true believers. Dreiser was naturally skeptical. He therefore asked that he
be allowed to remain in the Soviet Union for a longer period. He wanted to
travel and see the genuine, unofficial Russia. His hosts obliged him, though
reluctantly. He stayed until January 1928, visiting Moscow, Leningrad, Kiev,
Kharkov, Rostov, Baku, Sevastopol, Odessa, and many other locations.

His secretary and companion on these travels was a young American
woman named Ruth Epperson Kennell. She was a political pilgrim who had
converted to communism and now made her living by translating and editing
English-language texts for the state publishing house. She and Dreiser were
attracted to one another and fairly soon became lovers. She was indispensable
to him in his travels, arranging for him to meet people who were not approved
by his government hosts, dealing with language and money problems, and
taking notes on his conversations and visits to museums and historical sites.

Dreiser had begun his diary in longhand in New York on the day he
received the invitation from the Soviet government. He made more entries
while on the voyage to Europe and during stopovers in Paris and Berlin. But

the keeping of the diary became burdensome, so he asked Kennell to take over the labor for him. What is more, he made the unusual request that she keep the diary in his voice, using the "I" pronoun to mean him, not her. In effect he asked her to assume his identify. Initially Kennell found the task awkward but soon took to it. Much of the latter part of the diary was typed by her, in Dreiser's voice, on a portable typewriter that she carried on the journeys. Some of the material was dictated by Dreiser; the rest she composed herself. Dreiser continued to make holograph entries from time to time, but the bulk of the diary, during the last six weeks of the odyssey, was kept by Kennell.

Dreiser had difficulty taking this diary with him when he left the Soviet Union. Unbeknownst to him, Kennell had sent a carbon copy of the parts she had typed to her superiors at VOKS, the government agency which handled cultural relations with foreign visitors. The bureaucrats at VOKS were wary of the use Dreiser would make of the document after he returned to the United States. Eventually they did let Dreiser take the diary, and he had it with him when he arrived in New York in February. Probably Kennell leaked the diary to protect herself. Dreiser was not altogether impressed by what he was seeing in the Soviet Union, and he had been obstreperous and aggressive in questioning some of the officials he had met. What he wrote about the Soviet experiment, once he returned to the West, might not suit his hosts. Kennell must have felt it in her best interest to keep her superiors informed. The document she sent to them survives today in the State Archives of the Russian Federation in Moscow. Kennell also kept a second, secret diary in which she recorded her own private thoughts about Dreiser. This diary is not known to survive, but Kennell mentions it and draws upon it in her book *Theodore Dreiser and the Soviet Union*.[3]

What were Dreiser's intentions for his diary? Possibly he thought of it only as an *aide-mémoire* for a book he meant to write about his journey, rather like the travel notes he had kept on the trips described in *A Traveler at Forty* (1913) and *A Hoosier Holiday* (1915). The character of this Russian diary is different, however, from the jottings in those earlier journals. Dreiser sets down conversations in quoted dialogue and makes references that would have been plain to him but would have needed explanation to a reader. After he returned to New York in early 1928 he spent a good bit of time with the diary, taking Kennell's sections, which she had given to him in loose typed sheets, emending and augmenting them in his own hand, trimming them with scissors, and pasting them onto the leaves of the blue-bound diary that he had used for his holograph entries.

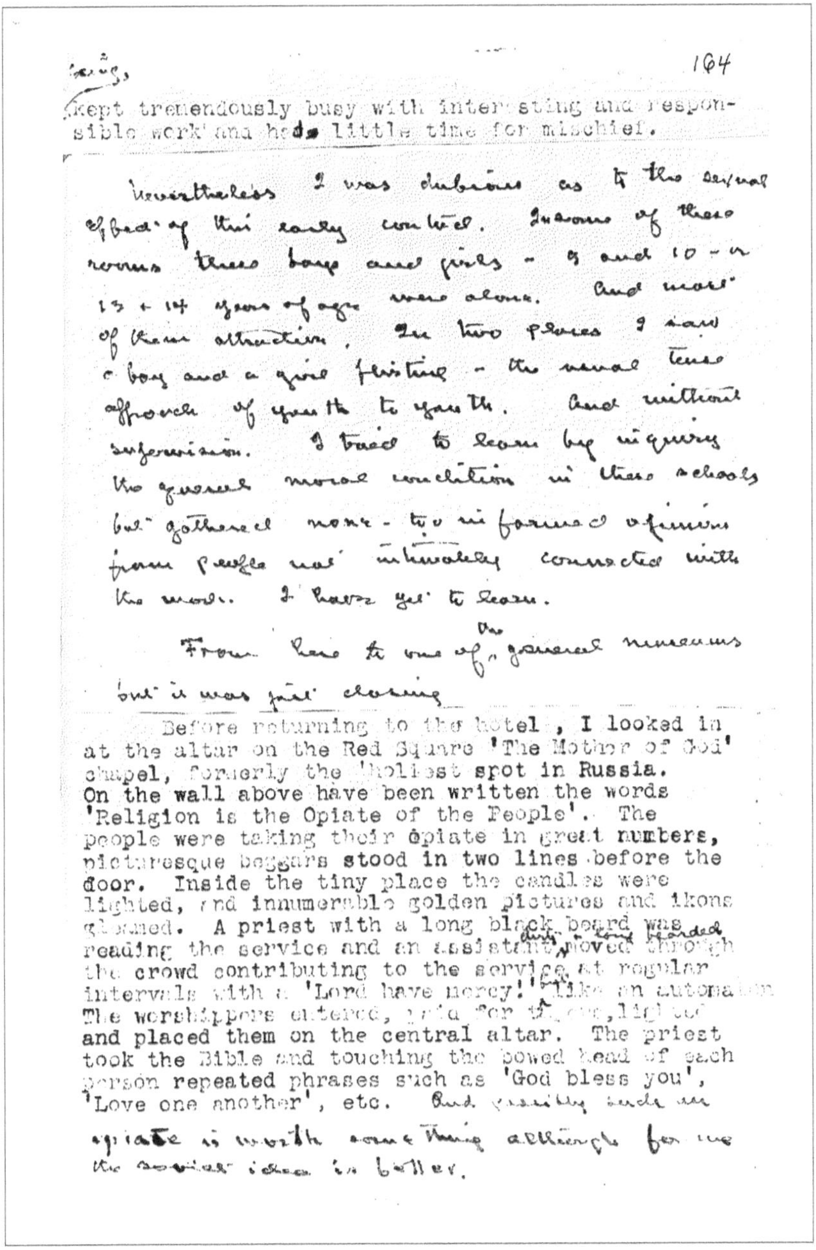

164

kept tremendously busy with interesting and responsible work and had little time for mischief.

*[handwritten insert:]* Nevertheless I was dubious as to the sexual effect of this early contact. In some of these rooms these boys and girls — 9 and 10 — 13 & 14 years of age were alone. And most of them attractive. In two places I saw a boy and a girl flirting — the usual tense approach of youth to youth. And without supervision. I tried to learn by inquiry the general moral condition in these schools but gathered none — too uninformed opinions from people not intimately connected with the work. I have yet to learn.

From here to one of the general museums but it was just closing

Before returning to the hotel, I looked in at the altar on the Red Square 'The Mother of God' chapel, formerly the holiest spot in Russia. On the wall above have been written the words 'Religion is the Opiate of the People'. The people were taking their opiate in great numbers, picturesque beggars stood in two lines before the door. Inside the tiny place the candles were lighted, and innumerable golden pictures and ikons gleamed. A priest with a long black beard was reading the service and an assistant moved through the crowd contributing to the service at regular intervals with a 'Lord have mercy!' like an automaton. The worshippers entered, paid for and lighted and placed them on the central altar. The priest took the Bible and touching the bowed head of each person repeated phrases such as 'God bless you', 'Love one another', etc. And possibly such an opiate is worth something although for me the soviet idea is better.

Fig. 3 Leaf 164 of Theodore Dreiser's Russian diary. The typed text is by Ruth Kennell, the handwritten insert and corrections by Dreiser. Theodore Dreiser Papers, Rare Book and Manuscript Library, University of Pennsylvania.

It's quite possible that Dreiser had plans to publish this document as a travel diary, a genre that was then popular. The surviving text shows indications of this intent, though Dreiser did not carry through with it. For some reason he abandoned his revising and never published the diary. Instead he took a shortcut, bringing together a series of articles that he had written for the *New York World*, revising and expanding them in places, and publishing the result as *Dreiser Looks at Russia* (1928). This is one of Dreiser's weakest books, a series of quickly written journalistic pieces that did little to advance his reputation. It is also the book for which he was accused of plagiarism by the journalist Dorothy Thompson, who believed that he had copied material from her book *The New Russia*.[4]

The accounts in the surviving Russian diary are much more revealing and vivid than those in *Dreiser Looks at Russia*. The diary includes colorful accounts of Dreiser's wanderings in Paris, where he met a young writer named Ernest Hemingway, and it contains his observations on the "large" personality, a figure who dominates his times by superior intellect and ambition. Dreiser met several such men in Russia and interviewed them: the cinema pioneer Sergei Eisenstein; the drama director Konstantin Stanislavsky; the political figures Vyacheslav Molotov, Vladimir Mayakovsky, Karl Radek, and Nokolay Bukharin. The diary records Dreiser's exchanges with them, plus interviews with lesser figures—party functionaries, local priests, workers in factories and communes. Certainly the diary needed to be put into print. It was one of the last documents of its kind from the 1920s and 1930s to remain unpublished. It deserved an audience and a continuing readership.

From the evidence on its pages, the Russian diary appears to fall somewhere between a public and a private document. With his handwritten revisions and augmentation, his cutting and pasting, Dreiser was bringing the diary into publishable shape. Whether he would have rewritten Kennell's sections is unclear, but if he had not then the published diary would have exhibited two very different textures and styles of prose. Perhaps Dreiser meant to have a rough copy made of the primary document, then to transform it into his own language, but this cannot be known, since he took his work no further.

Perhaps an editor should bring the text all the way into public form, carrying through on what were apparently Dreiser's intentions. Such an approach, however, would involve heavy correction and emendation and would produce a document still unfinished in organization and thought. It would encourage the diary to be interpreted as a fully realized work when plainly it is not. For these reasons it was judged improper to present the diary in public dress. The obvious course was to publish this Russian diary as a private document.

But how would Dreiser's parts of the diary, written in his own hand, be differentiated from the parts typed by Kennell? Several possibilities were available. The first was to set all of the text in the same roman typeface but to screen or shade Dreiser's parts. This would make readily apparent what he had written and what she had typed, but it would also create headaches for typesetters and would produce a text which looked "spotty" in the places in which Dreiser had only emended a word or a phrase here and there.

A second possibility was to employ two typefaces, a script face for Dreiser's handwritten parts and a typed face for Kennell's typescript texts. Compositors could indeed provide those faces, and two were selected for a sample. Parts of the book, especially toward the end of the diary, would be set almost exclusively in the typescript face. This would give the published volume the look of what used to be called a "typescript book," such as those published by companies specializing in secondary bibliographies and unrevised dissertations. These books were usually produced by shooting the image of the text directly from typescripts supplied by authors or checklist-makers. The volume that the University of Pennsylvania Press meant to publish was projected to carry an elevated retail price, too high for something that looked like a "typescript book." And, too, Dreiser's diary was an important document from a pivotal period of Soviet-American history; it deserved a type page that would invite close attention and serious reviews. Books set in typescript usually do not receive such treatment. The idea of using a typescript face for Kennell's sections was scrapped.

It was decided to use italic and roman faces, italic for Dreiser and roman for Kennell. This was the simplest approach and promised the fewest difficulties for the compositors. The diaries were set in "clear text," meaning that there were no symbols or diacritical marks to indicate canceled readings. Something was lost here, since it might be of interest to see what Kennell had first written and what Dreiser later substituted, but a careful reading of the text indicated that nothing significant would be sacrificed—only some changes in verb tense and pronoun reference. For the most part Dreiser had augmented her text, not changed it. A purist might object to the decision to print only the final readings, but the gain in readability overbalanced such criticisms.

The text was typeset, proofs were generated, and the checking began. The only problem, oddly enough, was the ampersand in the italic face. Dreiser used an ampersand in his handwriting, but it was a quickly inscribed mark resembling a plus sign. The ampersand in the italic face chosen by the book designers was an elaborate affair with swirls and curlicues. I should have noticed this problem on the typesetting sample, but I did not. The resulting text of Dreiser's handwritten entries is marred by these ampersands. If the aim of the edition was to reproduce the look of Dreiser's text as nearly as possible, then the ampersand was a sour note. Dreiser was jotting down these entries, recording his experiences and impressions with no thought of how the page would look. I asked whether the ampersands in the proofs might be changed to plus marks, perhaps by a global command, but I was told that the plus mark in this italic face took up much less em space than the ampersand. Substitution of plus marks throughout would cause the line endings to fall differently and make it necessary to create a new shooting copy for every page in the book, an expensive process that would require another round of proofing. The publication date was approaching. I settled for the ampersands, but in my view they disfigure the text. The lesson I learned was to pay more attention to preliminary dummies. On such small matters does an editor's satisfaction sometimes rest.

A much larger problem was the title page. What should the title of the book be? How should the byline read? These were important questions involving the collaboration between Dreiser and Kennell. The first page of the surviving document was headed "Russian Diary." Should the title page of the published book then read "*Russian Diary*" and the byline "by Theodore Dreiser"? Perhaps, but what of Kennell's contribution? Was she not the coauthor? Should the byline read "by Theodore Dreiser and Ruth Kennell"? Or perhaps "by Theodore Dreiser with Ruth Kennell"—rather like a ghostwritten book? Kennell had composed long sections of the diary in her own words, working from notes that she had taken, or from Dreiser's dictation; but she had done so in his employ (he paid her wages and expenses throughout) and at his direction. She had written in his voice, using his persona. Dreiser and Kennell had together created the physical text, but he possessed the document; he had cut and arranged and pasted her typescripts into the bound diary; he owned the document and its literary rights. Was this diary truly a collaborative performance?

Such considerations touched on gender politics. If the diary were published under Dreiser's byline alone, then would we be turning him into the kind of man who appropriates the ideas and labor of women in subordinate positions and presents them as his own? Perhaps, but he had done so before in his career, using the editorial talents of such women as Estelle Kubitz and (especially) Louise Campbell to help him put his writing into shape for publication. Those books were not published under dual bylines and had never been considered to be collaborations by biographers and scholars.

The final decision was to use no byline and to entitle the book *Dreiser's Russian Diary.* The possessive word "*Dreiser's*" has several meanings here. This was a record of Dreiser's journey; it had value because he was who he was. He caused the record to be kept; it was an account of what had happened to him, not to Kennell. She wrote parts of it, but under his instructions and in his voice. Finally, he owned the diary, the paper and ink and paste and binding. The possessive form seemed right. The book would be presented as an edition of the surviving document, of "Dreiser's Russian Diary," which had rested unpublished among his papers for almost seventy years.

This was not altogether satisfactory, but it seemed an acceptable compromise. I had hoped that the Library of Congress publication data on the copyright page might reflect Kennell's role in the making of the diary, perhaps listing her as a collaborator or assistant, but I learned that the Library of Congress has rules for the presentation of such data. One of these is that for a name to be listed in an authorial role, it must appear on the title page. Dreiser's name would appear on the title page because the book was to be published as "*Dreiser's Russian Diary.*" Kennell's name would not be there, so she could not be listed in the Library of Congress data.

By way of balancing the scales, Kennell was identified in the first paragraph of the preface as Dreiser's "secretary and companion for the trip," who "contributed significantly to the composition of the diary" (xi). Her role in its making was described clearly in the introduction, written by my co-editor, Thomas P. Riggio, and in the editorial principles section, composed by me. Riggio emphasized Kennell's importance to Dreiser as his first teacher about the realities of life in the Soviet Union; she argued politics and social theory with him and influenced him strongly in his final estimate of the Soviet experiment, a subject about which he would write from time to time for the rest of his career. Still, her name was not on the title page or copyright page. I wish it had been, but it was impossible to solve the question satisfactorily. Today, fifteen years later, I cannot see how matters might have been handled differently without creating other distortions and problems.

These three cases—from Dreiser's *American Diaries,* his *Russian Diary,* and his manuscript for *An American Laborer*—provide good examples of questions that the editors of private documents must face. Such editing is thought to be easier than the editing of novels, stories, and poems. Perhaps that is true, but private documents can still present knotty problems involving intention, authorship, arrangement, and emendation. Preparing an edition of a private document is not always, as the saying goes, a piece of cake.

## NOTES

1. Theodore Dreiser, *American Diaries, 1902–1926,* ed. Thomas P. Riggio; textual ed., James L. W. West III; gen. ed., Neda M. Westlake (Philadelphia: University of Pennsylvania Press, 1982); Dreiser, *An Amateur Laborer,* ed. Richard W. Dowell; textual ed., James L. W. West III; gen. ed., Neda M. Westlake (Philadelphia: University of Pennsylvania Press, 1983); *Dreiser's Russian Diary,* ed. Thomas P. Riggio and James L. W. West III (Philadelphia: University of Pennsylvania Press, 1996).

2. Richard Lingeman, *Theodore Dreiser: At the Gates of the City, 1871–1907* (New York: Putnam, 1986); Lingeman, *Theodore Dreiser: An American Journey, 1908–1945* (New York: Putnam, 1990).

3. Ruth Epperson Kennell, *Theodore Dreiser and the Soviet Union* (New York: International, 1969).

4. See Lingeman, *Theodore Dreiser: An American Journey,* 315–17.

# TOXIC WORDS AND THE EDITOR

Editors must sometimes deal with toxic language. Reprinted, restored, or previously unpublished texts can reveal prejudices or attitudes toward ethnicity, race, sexual preference, or gender that are not countenanced today. Editors of such texts often use prefaces and introductions to explain or excuse these revelations or to put them into historical context. Editors also hide embarrassing passages by cutting and emendation. These editors are crafting texts that will avoid trouble and be palatable to modern readers and reviewers.

Such problems often emerge with private texts—letters, journals, and diaries. In such documents the author is unbuttoned and unprotected. A good example is the journalist and social critic H. L. Mencken, who kept a personal diary at irregular intervals from 1930 to 1948, the year in which he suffered a debilitating stroke that prevented him from reading or writing for the remaining eight years of his life. The diary, which runs to some twenty-one hundred pages in typescript, was among the papers donated by his executors to the Enoch Pratt Free Library in Baltimore after his death. Under the terms of Mencken's will, the diary was sealed for twenty-five years after his demise, this to protect the reputations of people who were mentioned unfavorably in it. The diary was opened and inspected in 1981, but as it turned out many of these people were still alive. Mencken's executors decided to restrict access to the diary for several more years and to be careful about allowing anyone to quote from it.

During this waiting period, important matters were addressed. Did Mencken create this diary for publication? Would he have wanted it to be put into print after his death? A note signed by Mencken and attached to the document is ambivalent. It reads as follows: "This diary is to be deposited by my Executors on the understanding that it is not to be put at the disposal of readers until twenty-five years after my death, and is then to be open only to students engaged in critical or historical investigation, approved after proper inquiry by the Chief Librarian."[1] The note does not exactly forbid publication; it simply says that the diary should be seen only by people who might have a legitimate critical or historical interest in using it.

Enoch Pratt Free Library and Alfred A. Knopf, Inc., Mencken's publisher, sought an opinion in 1985 from the attorney general of the State of Maryland, Stephen H. Sachs, about the legality of publishing the diary. Sachs saw no reason why the document should not be made public, so plans went forward to make a representative selection of the entries, about one-third of the total, and to publish them in a single volume. (The full twenty-one-hundred-page manuscript would have made an immense book in printed form, full of repetitions and of much tiresome medical detail, for Mencken was a great hypochondriac.) An editor, Charles A. Fecher, was secured; Fecher was a respected Baltimore journalist who had written a good book on Mencken.[2]

The delays and the opinion from the attorney general, however, seem to have alerted the press that something was afoot. Were there passages in Mencken's diary that would not bear present-day scrutiny? Rumors began to circulate that the diary revealed a dark side of Mencken, a bleak, nihilistic persona not present in the published writings. There were also reports that the diary contained unenlightened remarks about Jews, African Americans, women, and other minority or marginalized groups.

*The Diary of H. L. Mencken,* running to some 475 printed pages, was published in the late fall of 1989 by Knopf. In the introduction Fecher attempted to address the rumors by noting that there was in fact no bitter, disillusioned Mencken hiding in the diary. The voice there is world-weary, but not overly so, considering Mencken's age and health. Fecher did admit, though, that by contemporary standards Mencken revealed himself to be anti-Semitic in the diary, that he showed a patronizing attitude toward black people, and that some of his comments about women were demeaning.

Fecher's editorial stance was apologetic. Earlier, in his own book on Mencken, he had defended the author against charges of anti-Semitism; now he admitted that he would probably rethink his position were he to address the issue again. Journalists were quick to pick up on this lead, in part because Fecher had furnished, in his introduction, several anti-Semitic passages from the diary. Thus it was not necessary to read the full volume in order to ferret them out. Newspaper reporters and reviewers in Washington, D.C., Chicago, Boston, and elsewhere created a controversy about the diary, giving the bulk of their attention to Mencken's anti-Semitism, which they treated as a hitherto unknown revelation. They wrote articles and columns about his attitudes toward Jews, arguing the issues back and forth and generating a good deal of intemperate exchange. The headlines suggest the tone of the writing. From the *Washington Post,* for example: "Mencken's Dark Side" (5 December 1989), "Reconsidering Mencken—Racism in Diaries Stuns Baltimore" (8 December 1989), "Mencken's Unsurprising Prejudices" (11 December 1989), "Gag the Yahoos?" (17 December 1989); from the *Boston Globe:* "Mencken Diary Reveals Racism" (5 December 1989), "Mencken's Sins, History's Judgment" (6 December 1989); and from the *Chicago Tribune:* "Mencken's Secret Diary Reveals Bigotry" (6 December 1989), "Dunderheads Target Unfair Mencken" (17 December 1989), "Mencken the Horrible" (17 December 1989). Some members of the National Press Club in Washington, D.C., wanted to rename the club's H. L. Mencken Library.[3] Eventually their proposal was defeated by a 7–4 vote, taken by the executive board of that organization in February 1990. The issue of Mencken's anti-Semitism stayed warm in the press until April 1990. After that it died out.

It is a revealing exercise today, more than twenty years later, to anatomize the reaction of the print media to Mencken's diary. The attackers used what might be called the "James Watt" approach. Watt was a former secretary of the interior who, in September 1983, made a thoroughly unenlightened remark about blacks, Jews, women, and disabled people in a speech delivered to the U.S. Chamber of Commerce. For that gaffe he lost his position in the cabinet. Since then a great many public figures have been similarly caught out. The reviewers and columnists who attacked Mencken implied that an American literary figure of high repute had exposed his hidden prejudices and been unmasked as an anti-Semite. Should he, like James Watt, be punished?

It might be thought that Mencken, long in his grave, would be beyond punishment, but the case of Paul de Man proves that this is not so. In fact, the exposure of de Man after his death as an anti-Semite might have had an influence on the reception of Mencken's diary. De Man was a Belgian who emigrated to the United States and eventually won a position on the faculty at Yale University. He became one of the major proponents of deconstruction, an approach to literary interpretation that had a considerable vogue during the 1970s and 1980s. A few years after de Man's death, it was revealed that in the early 1940s he had written numerous pro-Nazi journalistic pieces in *Le Soir,* a Belgian newspaper that was taken over by the Germans during World War II. Several of de Man's columns were strongly anti-Semitic.

The revelation of this information, about which de Man had kept silent during his life, broke in the *New York Times* on 1 December 1987, about two years before the publication of Mencken's diary; stories on the de Man case appeared in *Newsweek,* the *Nation,* and the *London Review of Books.*[4] David Lehman, a scholar and poet, wrote a book on the affair entitled *Signs of the Times: Deconstruction and the Fall of Paul de Man.*[5] The controversy dealt with whether de Man's pro-Nazi sentiments should influence how literary people were to regard deconstructionist thinking. Fascism and deconstruction have some things in common. Like fascism, deconstruction exhibits a strong element of nihilism and, in de Man's rendering of it, has much to say about the futility of words and the ultimate meaninglessness of language and human action. De Man's reputation and the status of deconstruction in the academy were both injured by the revelations, though it is impossible to say how deep or long lasting the injuries were.

The de Man controversy broke near the end of 1987 and continued to be an intermittent issue in the popular press and in academic journals well into 1989. Perhaps the journalists who attacked Mencken as an anti-Semite in late 1989 and early 1990 had the Paul de Man case in mind. Could a punishment similar to de Man's be arranged for Mencken? Revelations of hidden prejudices were powerful weapons in the canon wars of the 1980s and 1990s. Could Mencken be ejected or disbarred from the canon of American literature?

The problem was that Mencken had never really been *in* the canon. He was a journalist, critic, language scholar, editor, and man of letters generally; but he wrote no memorable fiction or poetry, which constitute most of what is taught in the standard English department curriculum. Mencken had never fit into the canon especially well and had not been much taught at the college level. His following had never been exclusively academic: most of his readers were (and are) among the laity. They read him for his opinions, which wear well and keep their pungency over time, and for his strong, distinctive prose style.[6] Banishment from the academic canon was not a realistic possibility. Attackers of the diary therefore expressed outrage over Mencken's bigotries and left it at that.

What about the anti-Semitic comments in the diary? Mostly they involve the use of the word *Jew.* A careful reading and marking of the published diary yields some thirty passages in which Mencken comments on Jews or uses the words *Jew* or *Jewess.* In the 1930s these words were not considered to be racist epithets in the same way that they are today. Many of the references, in fact, are neutral. One man is "a brisk, clever Jew" (55), another is "a young

Harvard Jew" (71); a woman is "a French Jewess" (55), another is simply a "Jewess" (106). Mencken speculates about a man who "looks decidedly Jewish" (114), mentions "two Jews" among the members of his Saturday Night Club (197), and remarks that someone is "not a Jew" despite a Semitic-sounding name (223). Marcella Powers, Sinclair Lewis's inamorata, is "a young Jewess" (162). A man in one of the entries is "the only Jew on the guest list" (324). Mencken praises the Baltimore city politician Simon E. Soboloff as "a smart Jew" (371) and writes that the medical journalist Morris Fishbein is "a shrewd Jew" whose "services to American medicine have been extremely valuable" (287). The attorney Leonard Weinberg, a member of one of the "richer Jewish firms in Baltimore," is "a highly intelligent fellow" whose "observations are always sharp and sound" (294).

Many of the derogatory references to Jews are remarks by others that Mencken is recording. An acquaintance tells him that the graduate students in the history department at Harvard are "mainly Jews" and that "few of them showed any capacity" (198). In reporting on a conversation with Dreiser, Mencken twice refers to Hollywood movie moguls as "the Jews" (47, 369). Dreiser tells Mencken that "a Jew named Pell," now in control of the bankrupt publishing house of Liveright, is "a fearful swine" (87, 117). A woman who owns a garment factory in Kansas City dislikes dealing with a workers' union because it is "operated by New York Jews" (137). Some passages in Mencken's own voice contain negative comments about Jews. He refers to a prominent family of newspaper publishers in Philadelphia as "the Annenbergs, who are low-grade Jews" (277). He calls the mass publisher Emanuel Haldeman-Julius "a highly dubious Jew" (302). He reports that Alfred Knopf realizes he has hired "too many Jews in his office" (422). A sales manager at Knopf is "a Jew, and moreover, a jackass" (317). After delivering a talk to the Stuart and Tudor Club, a literary society at Johns Hopkins, Mencken fielded questions from the audience. The questions irritated him. "It was obvious that most of the questioners were radicals," he writes, and "that many of them were Jews" (336). Frank R. Kent, a journalist friend, was uncomfortably "bracketed with two Jews" at the dinner table during a meeting of the Gridiron Club in Washington, D.C. (411). And Mencken records without approval or disapproval the story of a man named Winter who was voted into the Maryland Club, a private social organization, but was nudged out when his real name (Winternitz) and his ethnicity (Jewish) were discovered. In the past the Maryland Club had "always had one Jewish member" but now had none. "There is no other Jew in Baltimore who seems suitable," writes Mencken (286–87).

Curious to see whether there might be anti-Semitic passages stronger than these that were left out of the printed edition, I spent six hours on Friday, 28 May 1989, reading through the twenty-one-hundred-page typescript of the document in the Mencken Room at the Enoch Pratt Free Library. I did not read every entry in its entirety; instead, I looked carefully for text in which Mencken made remarks specifically about Jews. The unpublished passages that I found were of a piece with those in the published diary. I discovered no scurrilous or defamatory remarks about Jews that had been excluded from print. The references (published or unpublished) to Jews in the diary certainly betray anti-Semitism, but it must be said that these passages fail by a considerable margin to deliver the punch necessary to brand Mencken a genuine hater of the Jewish people or even a deeply committed anti-Semite.

Some of Mencken's defenders tried to argue that his anti-Semitism was more or less typical of his times or, inevitably, that many of his best friends were Jews—which, as it happens, they were. Mencken's anti-Semitism was not virulent or intemperate, and he did not hide it, as some journalists alleged. On a scale of 1 to 10, Mencken's anti-Semitism, as revealed in the diary and in his other writings, should be rated at about a 4 or a 5. Among American literary figures this is not an especially high score. Ezra Pound (in my estimation) heads the list with a 10; Henry Adams deserves a 9; Dreiser and T. S. Eliot both score 8s. Wharton earns a 7 and Hemingway a 6 (perhaps higher), Mencken a 5 or 4, Willa Cather a 3, and F. Scott Fitzgerald a 2. It would be fair to say that Mencken, for his time, was a middle-grade, garden variety anti-Semite.

Sometimes writers make it easy for editors by expunging prejudicial language from early texts when they are reset for later editions. This happened with Mencken's *Treatise on the Gods*, a study of religion originally published by Knopf in 1930. That edition contained the following passage: "The Jews could be put down very plausibly as the most unpleasant race ever heard of. As commonly encountered, they lack many of the qualities that mark the civilized man: courage, dignity, incorruptibility, ease, confidence. They have vanity without pride, voluptuousness without taste, and learning without wisdom. Their fortitude, such as it is, is wasted upon puerile objects, and their charity is mainly only a form of display" (345–46). Mencken drew heavy criticism in the Jewish press for the passage. A small controversy followed—which might have been Mencken's intent from the beginning, since he often baited ethnic, religious, or political groups in print. Alfred Knopf, himself a Jew, wrote to Mencken: "From what I hear around town I begin to think that a large proportion of Treatise sales are to the very Jews who are objecting so violently to that paragraph."[7]

*Treatise on the Gods* sold through ten trade impressions and stayed on the Knopf backlist until the early 1940s, when it fell out of print. In 1945 the publisher proposed a freshly typeset edition to Mencken, who agreed and took the opportunity to make changes in his text. He updated verb tenses, introduced references to recent events, inserted a few digs at FDR, whom he loathed, and put in some fresh cracks to offend the Methodists, who amused him. He softened the passage on the Jews, producing this revised version in the 1946 second edition: "As commonly encountered, [the Jews] strike other peoples as predominantly unpleasant, and everywhere on earth they seem to be disliked. This dislike, despite their own belief to the contrary, has nothing to do with their religion: it is founded, rather, on their bad manners, their curious lack of tact. They have an extraordinary capability for offending and alarming the *Goyim,* and not infrequently, from the earliest days down to our own time, it has engendered brutal wars upon them" (286). Had Mencken altered his opinion of Jews? Probably not, at least not substantially. But he was surely influenced in 1946 by reports that had begun to come in from eastern Europe during the previous year, exposing Hitler's programs of internment and genocide. Mencken's tendency in the early 1930s had been to treat Hitler as a clownish figure who posed no real threat to the balance of power in Europe. He could see now that he had been wrong. Hitler had been a fanatic and a murderer; the German people, whom Mencken had admired and praised, had been his accomplices. To have retained the offending paragraph from the 1930 text of *Treatise on the Gods* in the 1946 edition would have been unthinkable.

If one were to edit a new edition of *Treatise on the Gods* today, how would one handle this passage? Should Mencken be allowed his revision, or should it be rejected as a gesture that he made only for cosmetic purposes? If rejected, then what should the editor do with the numerous other revisions and updatings made for the 1946 edition? The most politic approach would be to print the softened 1946 passage, with the original 1930 text given in the apparatus or in a footnote. The same courtesy was extended to W. E. B. Du Bois by the scholar Henry Louis Gates Jr., who, in a Norton Critical Edition, called attention to anti-Semitic language in all printings of *The Souls of Black Folk* (A. C. McClurg and Co., 1903) executed before 1953. In the Fiftieth Anniversary Jubilee edition of the book published by Blue Heron Press, Du Bois replaced eight occurrences of the word "Jew," used in an invidious way, with "immigrant" or "foreigner" or "American" or "peasant." Gates accepted these changes for his new edition. If Du Bois can be allowed his revisions, then Mencken should be permitted his.[8]

How far can such editorial courtesies be stretched? Marion Mainwaring, an Edith Wharton scholar, wrote an ending for Wharton's *The Buccaneers,* which Wharton had left uncompleted at her death and which had been published as a fragment by Appleton-Century in 1938. Mainwaring's edition was published by Viking in 1993. In preparing the text for Viking, Mainwaring edited out the word "nigger." In her afterword she explained that she had made changes when Wharton "referred to race in terms offensive to modern readers" (407). A reference to "nigger songs" on page 158 of the Appleton edition becomes "Deep South songs" on page 129 of the Viking edition; "an amateur nigger-minstrel performance" on page 243 of Appleton is changed to "an amateur Negro minstrel performance" on page 200 of Viking. The words "Negress" and "octoroon" on pages 92 and 114 of the Appleton edition, however, are not altered.

In what one would suspect to be a piece of japery were it not presented so earnestly, an editor named A. S. Ash published, in 1992, a text of Walt Whitman's 1855 edition of *Leaves of Grass* with language purged of gender distinctions. Ash writes, "Whitman's language, though remarkably nonsexist for his time, has been humanized where appropriate (i.e., *human* or *person* substituted for *man* when the context clearly indicates no sexual reference is intended). Humanist personal pronouns (*hu, hus, hum,* pronounced *who, whose, whom*) have been substituted in cases where distinction of gender is ambiguous, irrelevant or misleading."[9]

In the case of Mencken's diary, Fecher might have chosen not to include anti-Semitic passages from the original. The problem was that Fecher was under pressure to include some of the anti-Semitic entries because of advance speculations in the press. In 1993, four years after the diary appeared, Jonathan Yardley, the editor of *My Life as Author and Editor,* another unpublished book left by Mencken at his death, wrote in his introduction that "the largest of Mencken's warts" for contemporary readers "is what they perceive as his anti-Semitism." About his editing of Mencken's manuscript, Yardley wrote: "I have made certain not to excise any material that might be unfavorable to Mencken in that regard. . . . To the best of my knowledge every word of it is included in this volume; no whitewash is intended or desired."[10]

In presenting a sizable body of material—a diary or an extended collection of letters from which one must make selections—an editor should probably choose representative examples of diary entries or letters that reveal prejudice. But what would be a "representative selection"? Exactly how anti-Semitic was Mencken? Thirty entries worth? Forty-five? How sympathetic (or not) was

William Faulkner toward African Americans? How misogynistic was Edith Wharton? How homophobic was Hemingway? Making decisions of this sort suggests that scholarly editing is not altogether a mechanical pursuit. The decisions facing the editor are whether to publish, what to publish, and how to introduce what is being put into print.

F. Scott Fitzgerald's writings offer some examples of nervous editing. In one of the most memorable scenes in *The Great Gatsby*, for example, Nick Carraway is at a party in the apartment on West 158th Street that Tom Buchanan maintains for his trysts with Myrtle Wilson. Tom and Myrtle have invited some friends to come in for drinks. Nick finds himself talking with Myrtle's sister, whose name is Catherine. This is a coarse crowd, not squeamish about what they say in conversation. Catherine brings up the liaison between Myrtle and Tom: "Neither of them can stand the person they're married to," she says in a loud voice. Mrs. McKee, a neighbor from elsewhere in the building, overhears the remark and, in the 1925 Scribner's first edition, reveals how she might herself have fallen into a bad marriage: "'I almost made a mistake, too,' she declared vigorously. 'I almost married a little kyke who'd been after me for years. I knew he was below me. Everybody kept saying to me: "Lucille, that man's 'way below you!" But if I hadn't met Chester, he'd of got me sure'" (41).

Most editions of *The Great Gatsby* since 1925 print either "kyke," Fitzgerald's spelling from the manuscript, or the more commonly found "kike." But within the first American paperback edition (published initially by Bantam Books in November 1945, five years after Fitzgerald's death), one finds a plate variant on page 42. The variant occurs between the third impression of March 1946 and the fourth of March 1951. The word "kyke" becomes "guy." As with Mencken's revisions for the 1946 *Treatise on the Gods*, one notes the date and wonders whether the revelations about the Nazi death camps and, more generally, public awareness of the suffering of European Jews during World War II might have prompted the change. There is a further twist: in the 1974 Penguin Books edition of *The Great Gatsby*, timed to appear with the premiere of the Paramount movie version starring Robert Redford and Mia Farrow, "kyke" becomes "tyke" (40). This alteration was carried forward into an undated Penguin Modern Classics resetting that is still for sale in the United Kingdom today.

Neither Bantam printing of *The Great Gatsby* includes a true textual note. The Bantam fourth impression of 1951, in which "kyke" becomes "guy," carries the following statement on the final page of the text: "This Bantam book contains the complete text of the original edition. Not one word has been changed or omitted" (191). Neither of the two Penguin editions (with "tyke") says anything about its text. The sentence does not offend as it should when "kyke" becomes "guy" or "tyke." Of course it is the vulgar Mrs. McKee who uses the word, not Fitzgerald or Nick, but for safety "kyke" was changed in both of these texts.

Other writings by Fitzgerald have been similarly altered. In a 1922 story entitled "Two for a Cent," set on a hot day in the South, Fitzgerald has a sour, disillusioned character named Abercrombie speak these two sentences: "'It's just that this is too damn hot to be a white man's country and it always will be. I'd like to see 'em pack two or three of these states full of darkies and drop 'em out of the Union.'"[11] Fitzgerald did not include "Two for a Cent" in any of his own short story collections, though it was included in a "best stories" volume with the two sentences unchanged.[12] But when "Two for a Cent" was reprinted in a collection called *The Price Was High* in 1979, the editor omitted the two sentences and signaled the deletion with four ellipsis points and this asterisked footnote: "Forty-one words have been omitted."[13] When I reprinted the story in the Cambridge edition of *Flappers and Philosophers,* I retained the sentences and made a note in the introduction about the language expunged from the earlier edition.[14] The editor of *The Price Was High* should not be faulted for excluding the two sentences. That volume was meant to bring some forgotten Fitzgerald stories (many of them quite good) back into print and to show that, even when Fitzgerald was writing for money, he wrote well. The two omitted sentences, fixed upon by an enterprising journalist or a bloody-minded reviewer, could have soured the reception of the book. It should make a difference that it was Abercrombie and not Fitzgerald who spoke the lines in the story, but in 1979 (and perhaps today) that would not necessarily matter. A racist slur is a racist slur.

Another Fitzgerald short story has an even more complicated history of expurgation. This is "A Snobbish Story," one of a series of five narratives about a teenaged character named Josephine Perry published by Fitzgerald in the *Saturday Evening Post* in 1930 and 1931. Josephine is a rich girl who lives with her parents in Lake Forest, Illinois. "A Snobbish Story" is set during the summer. Josephine is bored: the only activities available to her are the same tea parties, tennis matches, and amateur theatricals that she participated in during the previous summer. Because she is beautiful and can sing, Josephine has been asked to star in an amateur vaudeville revue at the country club. She wants more stimulation than the revue will provide, however, and becomes involved in a production called *Race Riot,* being mounted by the Chicago

Little Theatre, an avant-garde group in the city. Josephine wants to go slumming. She has begun a flirtation with a brusque, tough-talking reporter named John Boynton Bailey, who writes for the *Chicago Tribune* and is the author of the *Race Riot* script. Bailey invites Josephine to play one of the leads. He takes her to a meeting of the cast, where he describes the action of his play: "'Listen. The girl in the play is like you. This race riot is caused by two men, one black and one white. The black man is fed up with his black wife and in love with a high-yellow girl, and that makes him bitter, see? And the white man married too young and he's in the same situation. When they both get their domestic affairs straightened the race riot dies down too, see?'"[15] Josephine wants to know which part she will play. "You'd be the girl the married man was in love with," explains Bailey. "The white one?" asks Josephine. "Sure," answers Bailey, "no miscegenation in this play." Fitzgerald adds: "She would look up the word when she got home" (256). This last exchange, preserved in the only typescript of the story to survive (the typescript bearing Fitzgerald's final revisions), was removed at the *Post* and does not appear in the text published in the 29 November 1930 issue of that magazine.

A few pages later Josephine takes Bailey to meet her parents, who need to give their consent for her to appear in the play and from whom Bailey hopes to extract money to cover the production costs. Mr. Perry asks Bailey about the script. This passage of dialogue follows:

> "Your play is about that?"
> "Yes. And I got so interested in the nigger side of the story that the trouble was to keep it from being a nigger play. The best parts are all for niggers."
> Mrs. Perry flinched.
> "You don't mean actual negroes?"
> He laughed.
> "Did you think we were going to black them up with burned cork?" There was a slight pause and then Mrs. Perry laughed and said: "I can't quite see Josephine in a play with negroes."
> "I think you'd do better to cut out colored actors," said Mr. Perry, "anyhow, if Josephine's going to be in your cast. I'm afraid some of her friends might not understand."
> "I wouldn't mind," Josephine said, "so long as I don't have to kiss any of them."
> "Mercy!" Mrs. Perry protested. (262–63)

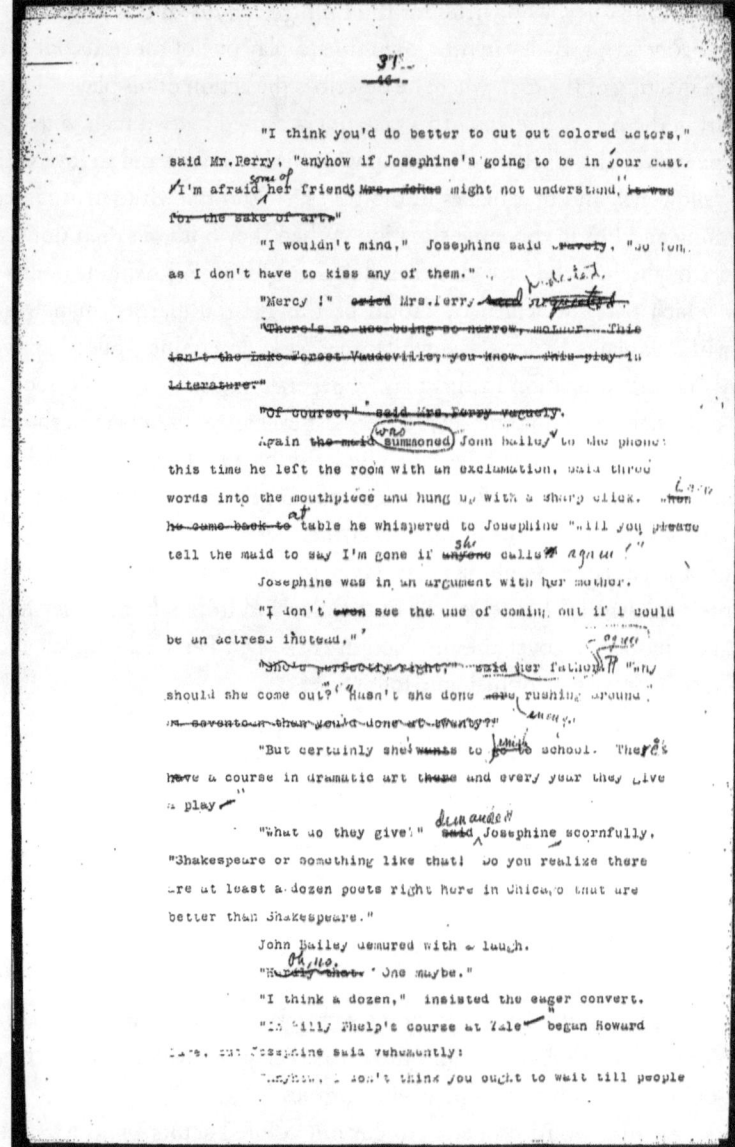

*Fig. 4* Leaf 31 from the working typescript of "A Snobbish Story," bearing Fitzgerald's handwritten revisions. The first seven lines were cut for the *Saturday Evening Post* appearance (29 November 1930). Reproduced with the permission of Harold Ober Associates, Inc., and Princeton University Libraries.

This text too was removed at the *Post*. The word "nigger" does survive in the *Post* text but only in a single sentence, earlier in the story. Bailey is telling Josephine about a colleague named Blacht. "Why, he's on the 'Tribune,'" says Bailey, "and he had to cover a nigger hanging this morning" (typescript and Cambridge text, 253). The *Post* printed this sentence but capitalized the word "Nigger." Magazine readers were therefore told about the plot of *Race Riot,* but the subject of miscegenation was avoided, and the skittishness of Mr. and Mrs. Perry about having Josephine appear on stage with black actors was absent.

Fitzgerald did not reprint "A Snobbish Story" during his lifetime. It did not have a second outing until it was included in a collection called *The Basil and Josephine Stories,* published in 1973.[16] Fitzgerald had included five of the Basil stories and three of the Josephine stories in *Taps at Reveille,* the last collection of short fiction that he published during his lifetime. For those stories, the editors of *The Basil and Josephine Stories* reprinted the collected texts. For the other stories, the editors reprinted the texts from the *Saturday Evening Post.* Consultation of manuscripts and typescripts at Princeton was outside the purview of their project. They reverted to a few readings from the *Post* when the readings in *Taps at Reveille* were confusing. As for the texts reprinted directly from the *Post,* the editors write that they "have made no silent corrections or emendations at all" (xxviii). This is not quite true. For "A Snobbish Story," one of the texts not reprinted by Fitzgerald, the word "Nigger" from the *Post* has been silently cut. The end of the sentence in the 1973 edition of *The Basil and Josephine Stories* reads, "he had to cover a hanging this morning" (255).

It is impossible to know what pressures the editors of *The Basil and Josephine Stories* were working under, whether the decision to eliminate the word "Nigger" was theirs or whether it was made by the publisher without their being informed. When I edited "A Snobbish Story" for the Cambridge Fitzgerald Edition, I returned to the typescript, the last form of the text known to have been revised by Fitzgerald, and restored all of the material dealing with race, including all occurrences of the word "nigger." The story is stronger for the restorations. The overt prejudices of Bailey (a representative of the press) and the covert prejudices of Josephine's parents (members of the Chicago haute bourgeoisie) are made apparent. Josephine, after her brief exposure to Bailey and his friends, decides that she will not associate with such people, nor does she want any contact with the problems of the underclasses. In the course of this single story, she encounters an open marriage (Bailey's), an instance of apparent adultery (by her father), lesbianism, racial prejudice, poverty, crime, capital punishment, and an attempted suicide (by Bailey's wife). Josephine has been coddled since birth. She wants nothing to do with unpleasant realities. Like Daisy and Tom Buchanan in *The Great Gatsby,* she has learned that the rich can withdraw behind barriers of status and money. In the last sentence of the story, Fitzgerald emphasizes this point. "Josephine decided something: That any value she might have was in the immediate shimmering present—and thus thinking, she threw in her lot with the rich and powerful of this world forever" (268).

Perhaps editors of scholarly texts have a duty to protect their writers from certain kinds of criticism. If the volume being edited is a selection of letters or a group of diary entries, then the editor can decide to omit most (or all) of the letters or entries that might create controversy, leaving them to be published if the complete texts are ever put into print. (If the editor chooses this rather dubious strategy, he or she should be prepared for negative reviews from scholars who have access to the original texts.) The option of benign bowdlerization is not available, however, to editors of public texts—of stories, novels, poetry, and nonfiction written deliberately for publication. For such writings the toxic words need to be retained or restored. Only then will readers and critics be able to come to a fair estimate of the views held by authors when they originally wrote the texts.

## NOTES

1. *The Diary of H. L. Mencken,* ed. Charles A. Fecher (New York: Knopf, 1989), xxi. The information in the paragraph that follows about the legality of publishing the diary is taken also from Fecher's introduction, xxi–xxiii.

2. Charles A. Fecher, *Mencken: A Study of His Thought* (New York: Knopf, 1978).

3. "Mencken Center May Be Renamed," *New York Times,* 13 December 1989, 22.

4. "Yale Scholar Wrote for Pro-Nazi Newspaper," *New York Times,* 1 December 1987, B1–B6; David Lehman, "Deconstructing de Man's Life: An Academic Idol Falls into Disgrace," *Newsweek,* 15 February 1988, 63; Jon Wiener, "Deconstructing de Man," *Nation,* 9 January 1988, 22–24; Christopher Norris, "Paul de Man's Past," *London Review of Books,* 4 February 1988, 8–11.

5. David Lehman, *Signs of the Times: Deconstruction and the Fall of Paul de Man* (New York: Poseidon Press, 1991).

6. Along these lines, see John Kenneth Galbraith, "Viva Mencken!" *New York Review of Books,* 28 June 1990.

7. Knopf to Mencken, 16 April 1930, Manuscripts Division, New York Public Library. Quoted in Mary Miller Vass and James L. W. West III, "The Composition and Revision of Mencken's *Treatise on the Gods,*" *Papers of the Bibliographical Society of America* 77 (1983): 454. See this article for a summary of the attacks on Mencken.

8. W. E. B. Du Bois, *The Souls of Black Folk,* ed. Henry Louis Gates Jr. and Terri Hume Oliver (New York: Norton, 1999), xl–xlii.

9. A. S. Ash, ed., *The Original 1855 Edition of "Leaves of Grass"* (Santa Barbara: Bandanna Books, 1992). See the review by Donald D. Kummings in *Walt Whitman Quarterly Review* 11 (Fall 1993): 86–89.

10. H. L. Mencken, *My Life as Author and Editor,* ed. Jonathan Yardley (New York: Knopf, 1993), xii.

11. Quoted from the serial text in *Metropolitan Magazine,* April 1922.

12. Edward J. O'Brien, ed., *The Best Short Stories of 1922* (Boston: Small, Maynard, 1923).

13. *The Price Was High: The Last Uncollected Stories of F. Scott Fitzgerald,* ed. Matthew J. Bruccoli (New York: Harcourt Brace Jovanovich, 1979), 38.

14. F. Scott Fitzgerald, *Flappers and Philosophers,* ed. James L. W. West III (Cambridge: Cambridge University Press, 2000), xxiii, 314.

15. F. Scott Fitzgerald, "A Snobbish Story," in *The Basil, Josephine, and Gwen Stories* (Cambridge: Cambridge University Press, 2009), 256. Subsequent quotations from the story, cited parenthetically, are from this text. For information about other editing at the *Post,* see the introduction, xviii–xxii.

16. F. Scott Fitzgerald, *The Basil and Josephine Stories,* ed. Jackson R. Bryer and John Kuehl (New York: Scribner's, 1973).

# DID F. SCOTT FITZGERALD HAVE
# THE RIGHT PUBLISHER?

Everyone knows that F. Scott Fitzgerald's publisher was Charles Scribner's Sons. F. Scott Fitzgerald, the Prophet of the Jazz Age, and Charles Scribner's Sons, one of the most staid, conservative, and prestigious of American publishing houses during the 1920s and 1930s—this has always seemed an improbable match, but no biographer or critic has ever suggested that the partnership was anything but happy and successful. Fitzgerald's biographers and critics, however, have focused almost exclusively on his relationship with Maxwell Perkins, the editor at Scribner's who discovered him and championed his work there. What of Fitzgerald's alliance with the publishing house? Was it healthy and successful? Was Scribner's the right publisher for Fitzgerald?

What kind of writer would Fitzgerald have become if he had allied himself with a different house? Would he have written the same novels and short stories? Would he have explored the same territory in his fiction? Addressed the same themes and adopted the same moral stances? A writer's publisher is not normally thought to influence such matters, but in Fitzgerald's case Scribner's almost surely did so. Scribner's had an important effect on Fitzgerald as a writer and a man—on his image, his style, his conception of his audience, his conception of himself, and his ethical position in his stories and novels. Charles Scribner's Sons, as a cultural entity, became an essential part of Fitzgerald's self-image, of how he defined himself as a writer, of the voice in which he spoke, and of the intellectual position from which he wrote. Scribner's was an integral part of Fitzgerald's creative apparatus.

Fitzgerald was attracted to Scribner's initially by the fact that it published, in America, the work of an Anglo-Irish writer named Shane Leslie. Fitzgerald had met Leslie while attending the Newman School in Hackensack, New Jersey, in 1912. The two had been brought together by Monsignor Sigourney Fay, the sophisticated prelate on whom Monsignor Darcy in *This Side of Paradise* (1920) is based. Fitzgerald came to know Leslie relatively well; Leslie was the first professional author to whom he had been exposed, and for a short time he was much under the spell of Leslie's writing and personal style. Leslie's American publisher was Charles Scribner's Sons; it was only natural that Fitzgerald, then sixteen, should also want to be published someday by Scribner's. The only other "real" author Fitzgerald knew was Henry Adams, to whom he had been introduced in Washington, D.C., also by Monsignor Fay. Adams, too, was a Scribner's author. This seemed to seal the issue: for Fitzgerald, if one wanted to be published, one should be published by Scribner's.

Many members of the Scribner family had attended Princeton. The original Charles Scribner had been a member of the class of 1840; his sons Charles and Blair and their sons Charles and Arthur had all taken degrees from the university since then. Most of the current editors and staff members at Scribner's were Princeton men, and there was a close relationship between the university and the publishing house. Scribner's had issued the writings of numerous members of the Princeton faculty, including those of Christian Gauss, Fitzgerald's mentor at the university. Scribner's had also been instrumental in founding Princeton University Press; in 1911 it had donated a building to the university to house the press.

Fitzgerald attended Princeton until 1917, when he left to serve in World War I. During his last semester he began writing a novel. By the spring of 1918 he had completed it under the working title *The Romantic Egotist*. He asked Shane Leslie to write a covering letter recommending the book to Charles Scribner, the head of the house, and to forward the manuscript to the New York office. Leslie did so, though apparently with some reluctance, and Scribner's received the manuscript in May 1918.

Fitzgerald had the good fortune to have *The Romantic Egotist* reviewed initially by Perkins, who recognized the potential in this young writer but saw that his manuscript was not yet ready for print. Perkins made Fitzgerald put the book through two revisions—the second one a major rewriting—before he would back it for publication. Charles Scribner was reluctant to take on the manuscript; Perkins insisted and eventually prevailed. Scribner's accepted the manuscript, now entitled *This Side of Paradise,* in September 1919. In his letter of acceptance to Fitzgerald, Perkins wrote, "I am very glad, personally, to be able to write to you that we are all for publishing your book. . . . I was afraid that, when we declined the first manuscript, you might be done with us conservatives. I am glad you are not."[1]

The two key words in Perkins's letter are "us conservatives." What did Perkins mean when he characterized Charles Scribner's Sons as a conservative house? Were the people at Scribner's conservative in politics and religion? Probably they were, but that is not what Perkins meant. He was referring instead to the business philosophy followed by his employers. Charles Scribner's Sons was deeply committed to the publishing strategies of the oldest and most traditional British houses—Murray, Constable, Bentley, Blackwood, Longman, and Macmillan. Their approach to the book business was based on price control and cooperation with one another. These British firms concentrated on small fields, or on groups of related fields, and published for a geographically limited and demographically similar market. Annual lists were relatively short; predictable sellers such as encyclopedias, textbooks, dictionaries, technical manuals, hymnals, and religious works provided the financial underpinnings for these houses. Such books subsidized gambles in fiction, poetry, and belles lettres. Overhead was kept low; advertising was limited and quiet in tone. The majority of sales came from the backlist, and many publishing decisions were made on the basis of how well titles could be expected to perform over the long term.

This approach had always worked well in Great Britain, a small and linguistically homogeneous territory that was well served by bookshops and an efficient rail service. Underselling and price-cutting had occasionally created problems for the British book industry, but for the most part the trade had been carefully regulated. It was more difficult to follow this approach in America, where the market was larger, more varied, and not as well organized; but a determined publisher could do so by treating the urban Northeast as the equivalent of Great Britain and regarding other sections of the country as the colonial market. This is the approach that Scribner's took to the book business. When we think of the firm in the 1920s and 1930s, we should think of a publishing house with a highly anglicized and essentially elitist business philosophy—operating, however, in democratic and egalitarian America. We should also think of a house that was most comfortable with a nineteenth-century approach to commerce—doing business, however, in the twentieth century. When Perkins wrote Fitzgerald to congratulate him on joining up with "us conservatives," that is what he meant.

In practical terms Fitzgerald's alliance with Scribner's meant that his publisher was reluctant to pay large advances on manuscripts or even to pay royalties ahead of time on strong-selling books. Charles Scribner would not issue contracts for unwritten books, nor would he negotiate multibook contracts. In his mind a publisher should be essentially passive about pursuing authors and manuscripts and should certainly not poach another firm's writers. He should concentrate on building the backlist and maintaining the reputation of the house. Appropriate authors and books would then come naturally to the firm. Charles Scribner had for many years refused to deal with literary agents. He had been forced to abandon this position by the time Fitzgerald became his author, but he still remained reluctant to negotiate with "author's representatives," as they were called. Fitzgerald obliged and never used an agent in arranging a contract with Scribner's.

The business philosophy at Scribner's, curious as it may sound, was not to make money. It was to avoid losing money. The thinking went this way: if most books sold well enough to cover their own production expenses, and if the books that lost money were prevented from losing too much, then one or two strong sellers each season, plus continuing and predictable sales from the backlist, plus occasional windfalls from reprint rights, would keep the firm in the black. To attempt to sell great numbers of books to the far-flung American reading public was unwise. For Scribner's it made more sense to stay close to home, concentrate on proven markets, and avoid spending money on extensive promotion or wide distribution. Money from the rights for stage and screen productions was welcome if it appeared, but the firm thought it undignified to market such rights aggressively. As a corollary Charles Scribner and his staff also believed it inadvisable (and perhaps impossible) for authors to support themselves solely with earnings from their books. Writers who tried to do so were often troublesome and importunate. Scribner's much preferred to handle authors who had other sources of income—Edith Wharton, for example, or Henry Adams or Theodore Roosevelt or Henry Cabot Lodge.

What commercial approach did Charles Scribner's Sons employ when it published one of Fitzgerald's novels? Let us examine the strategy used for *This Side of Paradise,* Fitzgerald's first novel, published in 1920. Its commercial history is representative of what one finds for any one of his subsequent books. Was Scribner's energetic in its marketing approach? Did it capitalize on the full sales potential of this much-discussed novel of the postwar generation? Did it collect significant money for the subsidiary rights? And did it handle the book in such a way as to make it generate long-term income for its author?

Like most publishers Scribner's was reluctant to take a chance on a first novel, even one that seemed certain to be popular. Sales of first novels were (and still are) unpredictable; it was best to manufacture a small first impression and wait to see how the initial orders and reviews went. This is how *This Side of Paradise* was published. The first impression was for only three thousand copies. This meant that when the many enthusiastic (and sometimes

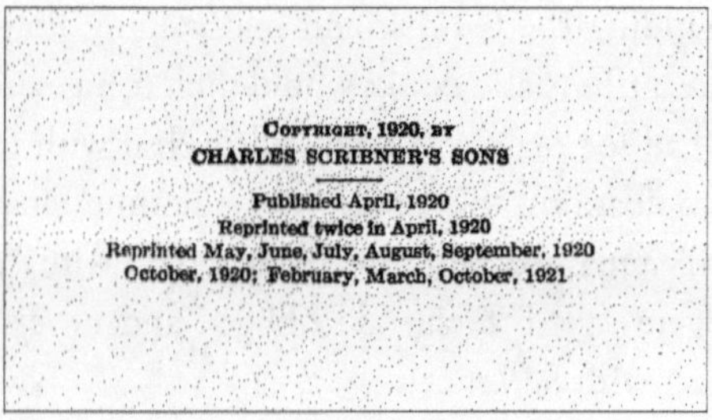

COPYRIGHT, 1920, BY
CHARLES SCRIBNER'S SONS

Published April, 1920
Reprinted twice in April, 1920
Reprinted May, June, July, August, September, 1920
October, 1920; February, March, October, 1921

*Fig. 5* Copyright page of the twelfth trade impression of *This Side of Paradise* (1920), showing the record of printings for the novel during its initial trade run. Collection of the author.

outraged) reviews of the novel appeared in the spring of 1920, there were not many copies of the book available in American bookshops.

*This Side of Paradise* would not have been an easy book to find on publication day—an understandable circumstance, since it was a first novel by a previously unknown writer. What is harder to understand, however, is that *This Side of Paradise* was probably something of a challenge to find throughout its trade run in 1920 and 1921. The usual procedure for a sales-minded house that finds itself with an unexpected hit on its hands is to rush out one or two large impressions so that the book remains in stock and reorders can be filled quickly. *This Side of Paradise* sold a little over 49,000 copies in its initial trade run: what one expects to see is a first impression of 3,000, followed by a second impression of perhaps 20,000, a third impression of another 20,000, and a fourth impression of 6,000 or so. Instead one sees a much more careful approach. There were twelve impressions of the novel between April 1920 and October 1921, all of them small. The first two were of 3,000 copies each; then followed seven of 5,000 copies each; then two more of 3,000; then a final impression of 2,000 in order to keep the book nominally in print.[2]

Scribner's played it safe throughout the trade run of *This Side of Paradise*. Their aim was to make some money (anyone could see that they were going to do this), but they did not attempt to realize the maximum amount that a novel such as *This Side of Paradise* might be expected to yield. The aim at Scribner's was to avoid losing money, which might have happened if someone had guessed wrong, ordered an overly large second or third printing, and seen the sales of the book end abruptly. Scribner's proceeded cautiously, ordering small reprintings as orders came in, probably running out of stock once or twice while the book was still hot, willing to lose some sales so long as the firm did not get caught in the end with a large unsold final impression that would clutter up the warehouse and eventually have to be remaindered. A more aggressive printing campaign, backed by strong advertising aimed at a broad national middle-class audience, would almost surely have sold a great many more copies of *This Side of Paradise.*[3]

Scribner's also realized relatively little money for the subsidiary rights. *This Side of Paradise* was not serialized or excerpted before publication, and its reprint edition was simply a binding-up of some leftover sheets by a remainder house. (There were no paperback reprinters, as we know them today, in the U.S. book trade during the 1920s. True paperback publishers did not appear until 1939.) Newspaper second-serial rights brought in a few hundred dollars; but stage rights, potentially much more lucrative, were never sold. Movie rights were not marketed until three years after publication, by which time the novel was no longer in the public eye. These rights brought in only ten thousand dollars, a low figure at a time when Sinclair Lewis's *Main Street,* also published in 1920, had fetched forty thousand dollars from Hollywood. Even so respectable a novel as Edith Wharton's *The Age of Innocence,* another novel published in 1920, had earned fifteen thousand dollars for its movie rights. The late sale of *This Side of Paradise* to Hollywood seems to have been an afterthought; not surprisingly, no movie version of the book was ever made. Scribner's did not seem to understand that there were numerous rights to resale and adaptation inherent in such a literary property. A popular work could be recycled in a variety of ways and made to yield steady income over a long period. Nor did Scribner's seem to think of *This Side of Paradise* as an especially important addition to its backlist. The house did keep the book nominally in print but made no effort in later years to reissue it (in an anniversary edition, for example) or to manipulate its reprint rights for extra money.

The patterns that emerge from a study of the Scribner business records, preserved at Princeton University Library, demonstrate that the approach used for *This Side of Paradise* was more or less typical of the strategy employed for all of Fitzgerald's novels. Scribner's never attempted to realize maximum or continuing income from his books, nor did it promote his subsidiary rights imaginatively or energetically. The directors protected their firm first. They proceeded cautiously and, as a result, probably never pushed Fitzgerald's books to their full commercial potential. All the same, they never lost money on a Fitzgerald book. They always covered their own expenses and made some profit for themselves and for Fitzgerald. What they failed to do was to generate substantial or continuing income for him.

This failure was responsible for Fitzgerald's reliance on the commercial magazine market for the bulk of his money. His total book earnings during his career, including subsidiary income, came to $74,500. His total earnings from the magazines for this same period totaled almost $312,000.[4] He was required to turn out short stories regularly for the *Saturday Evening Post, Hearst's International, Woman's Home Companion,* and other mass-circulation magazines to earn immediate money. This dependence on the slick magazines for income drained him and made it difficult for him to finish his novels, especially *Tender Is the Night,* which he finally completed after a nine-year struggle that left him physically and creatively exhausted.

Were there other publishers in the 1920s and 1930s who could have done better commercially with Fitzgerald's books? The most obvious possibility would have been Boni and Liveright, a natural house for Fitzgerald, at least at the beginning of his career. It was modern and freewheeling, at odds with the intellectual establishment, and experienced in handling such bestsellers as Warner Fabian's *Flaming Youth* (1923) and Anita Loos's *Gentlemen Prefer Blondes* (1925). But Horace Liveright, the head of the house, was irresponsible about his backlist and was inclined to risk money on Broadway productions and on the stock market. In need of capital, he sold off the Modern Library series to Bennett Cerf and Donald Klopfer in 1925, thereby losing his financial safety net. His firm went belly-up in 1932, leaving Theodore Dreiser, Sherwood Anderson, Eugene O'Neill, Robinson Jeffers, and many other authors stranded. It is fortunate that Fitzgerald did not go with Boni and Liveright, however good such a match might have looked in the early 1920s.[5]

That still leaves three good possibilities: S. S. McClure, D. Appleton and Co., and Doubleday and Co. McClure had a large fund of venture capital and close tie-ins with the magazine market. The executives there understood large-scale book distribution, knew how to promote bestsellers, and were not averse to dealing with literary agents. D. Appleton and Co. was doing an excellent job for Edith Wharton, who had left Scribner's in frustration over its anemic promotion of her books. Appleton might have done similarly well for Fitzgerald. It knew how to orchestrate the publication of a popular book, and it was arranging lucrative deals for Wharton's serial, drama, and movie rights. And the imprint was prestigious, even older than the Scribner imprint. Doubleday and Co. was probably the best possibility. Frank Doubleday foresaw the future of American book publishing more clearly than any other publisher of his generation. He had built up a large distribution network in America during the period just before Fitzgerald began his career, and he had immediate access to the British market through the Heinemann imprint in London, which he had acquired in 1920. He would establish the Literary Guild Book Club in 1926; his son, Nelson, would build it into a great success during the 1930s. Doubleday and Fitzgerald would have been a good match, as would McClure and Fitzgerald or Appleton and Fitzgerald. Any one of these three houses would probably have generated considerably more income for Fitzgerald than Scribner's did.

I am not lamenting the fact that Scribner's was Fitzgerald's publisher or suggesting that it mishandled his career or wishing that he had somehow landed with McClure or Appleton or Doubleday. Instead I am explaining how the business philosophy of a publishing house can affect an author's work and career—how that author must write to make money, reach an audience, and create a reputation. This is an appropriate inquiry with any writer but seems especially so for Fitzgerald, who was fascinated by money and its possibilities and was stimulated by success and public exposure. I am suggesting that, from a strictly financial standpoint, Scribner's was not the ideal publisher for Fitzgerald.

Would F. Scott Fitzgerald have been a significantly different writer if he had been published by another house? I believe that he would have been. I believe that he would not have written *The Great Gatsby* or *Tender Is the Night* as we have them, nor would he have written the short stories and occasional writings for which he is famous today. There would probably have been a generic similarity between the writings of the F. Scott Fitzgerald we know and the hypothetical F. Scott Fitzgerald who wrote for Liveright or Appleton or Doubleday, but that is all. Charles Scribner's Sons was much more than an imprint to Fitzgerald, more than an anonymous manufacturer and distributor of his books. The firm embodied a tradition and a set of standards that both attracted and repelled him. Several of the ethical problems that Fitzgerald addresses in his best novels—*The Great Gatsby, Tender Is the Night,* and especially *The Last Tycoon*—are intimately bound up with what Charles Scribner's Sons stood for.

For Fitzgerald, Charles Scribner's Sons meant the Newman School, Monsignor Fay, and Shane Leslie. Neither Fay nor Leslie had taken Fitzgerald seriously. Fay had enjoyed his company but had not believed in his potential as a writer, and Leslie thought of him as a callow American youth who could not spell correctly. Fitzgerald surely knew this or sensed it; that is why his considerable success with the very house that published Leslie's writings must have gratified him. It must also have pleased him that he was a popular author for Scribner's while Leslie never became more than a midlist writer there.

Charles Scribner's Sons also meant Princeton University. The strong connection between Princeton and Scribner's reached back over three generations. The much shorter connection between Fitzgerald and Princeton was tenuous and vexed. Three generations of Fitzgerald's forebears had *not* gone to Princeton. His maternal grandparents were Irish immigrants to America, and his mother and father were middle-class Catholics living in St. Paul, Minnesota—the wastelands of the American Midwest, so far as Princeton was concerned. Fitzgerald was the first member of his family to attend any university. He managed to last at Princeton for about three years; he stirred up the place a little while he was there, but he made no real mark. He almost failed to be admitted, failed to stay off academic probation, failed to win the honors he aspired to, and failed to take a degree.

From Fitzgerald's standpoint Princeton had failed him, and he was not afraid to say so. Parts of *This Side of Paradise* are highly critical of the university and of its stodgy approach to undergraduate education. In the first flush of his literary success he quarreled through the mails with the president of the university, John Grier Hibben, and he made flippant remarks about Princeton's country club atmosphere in interviews. He returned to his Princeton eating club, the Cottage Club, for a weekend in the spring of 1920, but he behaved badly, drinking more than he should have and getting a black eye in a fistfight. As a result he was banned from the club for an indefinite period. The experience soured Fitzgerald on Princeton for a time, and he did not return to the university for several years.

Yet Fitzgerald loved and admired Princeton—its lazy beauty, aristocratic ease, social stability, and air of rectitude. One part of him wished profoundly that he had fit in there and had been successful as an undergraduate. Another part, however, knew that his motivation and drive depended in important ways on his having failed at Princeton, that he wrote well about Princeton (and about the level of society that Princeton represented) precisely because he had been an outsider and a failure at the university.

For much of his career Fitzgerald was estranged from Princeton, but he did maintain one important link with the institution—Charles Scribner's Sons and all that the house represented. If Princeton was cool toward him, Scribner's was not. If he had been a failure at Princeton, he was a success at Scribner's. The things Fitzgerald had to say about Princeton had appeared under the imprint of Charles Scribner's Sons. It would not have been the same if Fitzgerald had spoken out in a book published by Liveright or Doubleday or McClure. His remarks about Princeton in *This Side of Paradise* were in-house criticism.

What else did Charles Scribner's Sons mean to Fitzgerald? One should try to imagine him throughout his career meeting people socially, encountering the alumni of other colleges on his trips to New York City, being introduced to other writers at Shakespeare and Co. in Paris, running into wealthy Americans there at the Ritz Bar, talking with movie people in Italy and on the French Riviera. In the course of the social preliminaries, it would be revealed that Fitzgerald was a writer. (Many of the people he met, of course, would already have known this.) Fitzgerald would probably be asked to recite the titles of the books he had published. Then, quite frequently, must have come a moment he rather looked forward to, the moment at which he was asked to name the house which published his work. The moment would be quite similar to the point at which an American academic is asked to name the college or university at which he or she teaches. Fitzgerald could answer the writer's version of this query with "Charles Scribner's Sons," words that would have suggested substance and tradition to almost any educated American of his generation.

That imprint meant a strong tradition of book publishing and a deep backlist. It meant William Cullen Bryant, Sidney Lanier, George Washington Cable, and Thomas Nelson Page. It meant Henry Adams and George Santayana; Theodore Roosevelt, Henry Cabot Lodge, and Whitelaw Reid; John Galsworthy, James Barrie, and Robert Louis Stevenson; Leo Tolstoy and Maxim Gorky; Henry James, Harold Frederic, and (until the 1920s) Edith Wharton. It meant *The Sacred Fount* and *The Wings of the Dove, The House of Mirth* and *Ethan Frome, The Last Puritan* and *The Forsyte Saga*. It meant *Scribner's Monthly*, with its dull yellow covers and its vaguely British contents. It meant the most handsome bookshop in New York City—the Scribner Bookstore at 597 Fifth Avenue. It meant James Hasting's five-volume *Dictionary of the Bible,* Henry Adams's nine-volume *History of the United States of America,* and Allen Johnson's twenty-volume *Dictionary of American Biography,* all monuments of scholarship. It meant the New York Edition of Henry James, a monument of a different but no less impressive kind. During the late 1920s and '30s, Charles Scribner's Sons also meant Ernest Hemingway, Ring Lardner, Don Marquis, Zona Gale, Thomas Boyd, Robert Sherwood, Thomas Wolfe, and Marjorie Kinnan Rawlings. This was an impressive set of associations.

What of Fitzgerald's own work? Being published by Scribner's, I believe, influenced quite strongly the voice in which he wrote and the authority with which he spoke. Being a Scribner's author became a significant part of his self-concept. I have no way of proving it, but I believe that Fitzgerald would not have written as confidently or acutely about American class structure, old and new money, or the nuances of social behavior if had he not been published by Scribner's. He might have been the Prophet of the Jazz Age, but like any prophet he needed credibility. His alliance with Scribner's validated what he had to say, gave him courage to speak, and imparted authority to his voice and vision.

One of the things that makes Fitzgerald's work fascinating is the way it balances between the diverting and the serious, the iconoclastic and the traditional, the entertaining and the profound—that is to say, between commerce and art. Fitzgerald walked a tightrope between commercialism and intellectual respectability all through his career; as readers we feel the tensions generated by his balancing act. We are a circus audience watching a skilled aerial artist teeter on a high wire overhead. We believe that our tightrope walker knows his business and that even his missteps and wobbles are practiced, but we are never sure until he completes his performance and descends to the ground. Would Fitzgerald have been an equally skilled high-wire walker if he had published with a different house? Would the same tensions between art and commerce have been present in his work? I believe that they would *not* have been, that Fitzgerald would probably have found his aerial act overly difficult and would have allowed himself to indulge his facility for the lightweight and flashy. He would have settled for something safer—stylish acrobatics on the ground, flips and handstands and cartwheels in the sawdust ring.

Finally we might consider ways in which Fitzgerald's relationship with Scribner's made its way into his fiction. Some of the problems he tackled in his work are similar to problems that faced Scribner's in the conduct of its publishing business. These were cultural dilemmas of the postwar era, recognizably American problems brought on by technology, urbanization, and prosperity. One finds them, then and now, in education, politics, religion, economics, and private life. For American businessmen these problems took the form of a series of choices: whether to adapt to new technology and automated manufacturing, whether to go after larger markets, whether to sacrifice quality for productivity, whether to enter into the cycle of heavy advertising and wide distribution, whether to measure success by one's reputation and code of ethics or by one's net income.

Because Charles Scribner's Sons was a business, it faced these choices. Would the house alter its nature, change its basic philosophy of publishing? Would it attempt to inflate its books into bestsellers by loud advertising? Would it abandon its responsibility to the literary culture and chase after popular authors from other houses, cut deals for serial rights with literary agents, pay large advances on multibook contracts, pursue book club sales, exploit stage and movie rights, expand its distribution network, begin to explore paperback publishing and book club distribution? It would not. Charles Scribner's Sons would remain a resolutely conservative and traditional business, convinced of the correctness of its course and the wisdom of its commercial practices.

The same kinds of choices face some of the characters in Fitzgerald's fiction. In *The Great Gatsby* Nick Carraway works in the bond-selling business, a pursuit in which fiscal conservatism, fair dealing, and responsibility to the larger society are not of the first importance. Socially Nick finds himself involved with careless, unethical people: with a graduate of Yale who cheats on his wife, a young woman who cheats in golf tournaments, and a former belle from Louisville who slides away from her moral responsibilities.

In *Tender Is the Night* Dick Diver lives in a world in which good manners, professional accomplishment, and ethical standards are considered to be superficialities. In the expatriate society that Dick inhabits, one can behave as irresponsibly as one wants to if one is rich enough. Dick Diver would have understood the business choices that were being made at Charles Scribner's Sons; Baby Warren, his sister-in-law and foil in the novel, would not have. Baby would have been contemptuous of the scruples at Charles Scribner's Sons. Dick's tragedy is that he must live in Baby's world, and the broader tragedy of *Tender Is the Night* is that Nicole Diver, Mary North, and even Rosemary Hoyt adapt themselves to Baby's standards and feel comfortable with them. Abe North does not; he is destroyed. Dick Diver cannot adjust either; he will be drained and discarded.

The character in Fitzgerald's fiction who most clearly embodies the dilemmas facing Charles Scribner's Sons is Monroe Stahr, the talented movie producer in the unfinished novel *The Last Tycoon*. Stahr, like his prototype Irving Thalberg, seeks to create movies of lasting artistic merit, but he also tries to make entertaining movies that people will want to see. Stahr is an artist at handling people, a master at coaxing popular films out of creative personalities, a juggler of money and minds and resources. He recognizes his responsibilities to the balance sheet but is even more conscious of his responsibilities to American culture. We know from the outline Fitzgerald left for the unwritten parts of *The Last Tycoon* that Stahr would eventually have paid a heavy price for his high standards. He would have been ousted by the money moguls in Hollywood who did not share his concern for artistic respectability.

The tensions between art and commerce facing Stahr in Hollywood are the same ones that Scribner's faced in New York. Fitzgerald encountered them in dealing with Scribner's and confronted them in his own work. He and his publishers were working the same ethical and cultural territory. Fitzgerald might not have been able to deliver a lecture on how the American book trade was organized, but he was aware of the choices that his publisher was making. He understood the book business as it applied to him. He knew exactly what kind of house Charles Scribner's Sons was and what kind of marketing effort he was getting. He discussed publication and sales strategies intelligently in his letters to Perkins and displayed a sharp awareness of the value of subsidiary rights in his correspondence with his fellow authors. He must have talked shop frequently with other writers and literary people; perhaps they asked him why he continued to publish with a house like Scribner's. We have no record of his answer. His answer is what I have been trying to reconstruct here.

Even with the most accurate hindsight and the strongest revisionist tendencies, it is difficult to feel regret over Fitzgerald's decision to stay with Scribner's. It is hard to imagine him publishing with a house that would have sold his novels aggressively, promoted his subsidiary rights cleverly, managed his earnings for him, put him on an allowance, kept him healthy, and made it possible for him to write the three or four additional novels that he probably had in him. It is impossible to picture a methodical F. Scott Fitzgerald punching in at his writer's time clock every morning, doing his daily three-hour stint before noon, then consulting with his agent after lunch over serial offers and book club opportunities and finishing the day by clipping coupons from his stock portfolio.

Fitzgerald did not live his life that way. The way he chose was self-destructive, but he realized, in the best romantic fashion, that this self-consumption fueled his art. "I wanted to grow old + live + break," he wrote to H. L. Mencken in 1935, and that is what he did.[6] The Fitzgerald we have come to know could not have been the methodical, solvent writer I have just described. Without the pressure of debt he might indeed have written several more novels, but they might well have been of little consequence—stylish but predictable. As it was, published by a resolutely conservative house and chained to the big-circulation magazines, Fitzgerald managed to write *This Side of Paradise*, *The Beautiful and Damned*, *The Great Gatsby*, *Tender Is the Night*, and a dozen or so of the best stories and essays of his time.

Did F. Scott Fitzgerald have the right publisher? Of course he did. With any other house he would have been a different writer, a good one, surely, but not the one we so much admire today.

NOTES

1. *Dear Scott / Dear Max: The Fitzgerald-Perkins Correspondence,* ed. John Kuehl and Jackson R. Bryer (New York: Scribner's, 1971), 21.

2. The dates and press-run numbers of the printings are recorded in Matthew J. Bruccoli, *F. Scott Fitzgerald: A Descriptive Bibliography,* rev. ed. (Pittsburgh: University of Pittsburgh Press, 1987), entry A5, pp. 14ff.

3. A good example of overly sanguine publishing is the mystery story *The Young Visiters,* written by a nine-year-old British girl named Daisy Ashford, and preserving her errors in spelling and grammar, as the title suggests. The book was issued by the American publisher George H. Doran in 1919 in a first printing of five thousand copies. A rumor started that the actual author of the novel was J. M. Barrie, and the book became a bestseller. Doran overreacted. He told the story years later in a memoir: "As quickly as printers and binders could manufacture, we produced exactly 250,000 copies. We sold 200,000, and at this point a fickle public decided to have no more of it and the sale ceased with the abruptness of a guillotine decapitation. Finally the ten-cent stores slowly disposed of what was left." Doran, *Chronicles of Barabbas, 1884–1934* (London: Methuen, 1935), 160. *This Side of Paradise* was speckled with errors in orthography and grammar. To his chagrin, Fitzgerald found himself being referred to in newspaper articles as "the Princeton Daisy Ashford."

4. Matthew J. Bruccoli, *Some Sort of Epic Grandeur: The Life of F. Scott Fitzgerald,* 2nd rev. ed. (Columbia: University of South Carolina Press, 2002), 523. The figures are compiled from Fitzgerald's professional ledger, a record of literary earnings that he kept for tax purposes.

5. In late May 1925, Fitzgerald received a letter from T. R. Smith of Boni and Liveright, asking whether he might be interested in leaving Scribner's. Fitzgerald feared that Smith might start rumors and wrote back immediately to insist that he had no desire to change publishers. Fitzgerald reported on the matter to Perkins in a letter of 1 June: "I answered at once saying that you were one of my closest friends and that my relations with Scribner's had always been so cordial and pleasant that I wouldn't think of changeing publishers." Fitzgerald elaborated later in the letter: "Tho, as a younger man, I have not always been in sympathy with some of your publishing ideas, (which were evolved under the pre-movie, pre-high-literacy-rate conditions of twenty to forty years ago), the personality of you and of Mr. Scribner, the tremendous squareness, courtesy, generosity and open-mindedness I have always met there and, if I may say it, the special consideration you have all had for me and my work, much more than make up the difference" (*Dear Scott / Dear Max,* 107–8).

6. Fitzgerald to Mencken, ca. 6 August 1935, in *Correspondence of F. Scott Fitzgerald,* ed. Matthew J. Bruccoli and Margaret M. Duggan (New York: Random House, 1980), 422.

# THE INTERNAL CHRONOLOGY OF
## *TENDER IS THE NIGHT*

Most of the attention given to the textual history of F. Scott Fitzgerald's 1934 novel *Tender Is the Night* has been devoted either to the story of its composition or to the author's "final version" published by the critic and editor Malcolm Cowley in 1951. Both of these matters have bearing on the internal chronology of the narrative. It will therefore be useful at the outset to give an account of the making of *Tender Is the Night* by Fitzgerald during the years 1925–34 and to describe its remaking, in Cowley's hands, for the 1951 edition. At issue is the strategy used to edit *Tender Is the Night* for the Cambridge Fitzgerald Edition. The internal chronology of the novel is the most important of the matters that an editor must address before commencing work on the text.

Fitzgerald began composing *Tender Is the Night* in the late spring of 1925, not long after publication of *The Great Gatsby* on 10 April of that year. In the earliest surviving drafts, *Tender Is the Night* was a novel of matricide, based loosely on a sensational tabloid murder that had occurred in San Francisco in January 1925. A sixteen-year-old girl named Dorothy Ellingson, angry because she had been forbidden to attend wild "jazz" parties, had shot and killed her mother on the morning of Tuesday, 13 January. After a long and dramatic trial she was convicted of manslaughter and sentenced to ten years in prison. Fitzgerald, who was living in Paris, followed the trial from wire reports published in the English-language newspapers available in the city.[1] He worked on this early version of his novel for several months but found the matricide plot alien to his temperament and put aside what he had written. Over the next four years he took up the matricide version at irregular intervals, twice trying to recast it from a first-person point of view. He abandoned all work on the novel during 1929–31, years in which Zelda Sayre, his wife, began to deteriorate mentally and required extensive hospitalization and treatment.

In 1932 Fitzgerald gathered his energies and developed a fresh plan for his novel. The new approach allowed him to salvage much of what he had already written, and by working steadily he finished *Tender Is the Night* in 1934. During these final two years he was living in Baltimore, where Zelda was a patient at a Johns Hopkins clinic. Her breakdown and hospitalization provided Fitzgerald with the impetus he needed to recast the novel. He transformed the protagonist, Dick Diver, into a psychiatrist, and Dick's wife, Nicole, into a victim of incest and (in consequence) schizophrenia. *Tender Is the Night,* now quite different from its beginnings as a novel of matricide, became a study of the disintegration of a talented but flawed man against a background of wealth and corruption in the American expatriate community of postwar Europe.[2]

*Tender Is the Night* was serialized in *Scribner's Magazine* in four installments, January–April 1934. The novel was published in book form by Charles Scribner's Sons on 12 April 1934. Reviews were mixed and sales moderate— around thirteen thousand copies. Fitzgerald was greatly disappointed. He had hoped that *Tender Is the Night* would earn money, give a boost to his career, and establish him as one of the most highly respected writers of his generation. Suffering from personal ills and creative failures, Fitzgerald entered what has come to be known as his Crack-Up period. He struggled professionally for three years and was only rescued by a contract that sent him to Hollywood in the summer of 1937 to work as a screenwriter for Metro-Goldwyn-Mayer. He held that job for eighteen months, then resumed work as a freelance in January 1939. Two years later, in December 1940, he died—with a novel under way that was eventually published in unfinished form as *The Last Tycoon* (1941).

In May 1936, one of the worst months of his Crack-Up, Fitzgerald conceived a plan to have *Tender Is the Night* republished with major alterations. This, he thought, would stimulate discussion of the novel and give it new life. He proposed to shift about large sections of narrative material in order to alter the structure of the novel. The 1934 text had been arranged in three books, the second of which is a long flashback giving a history of Dick Diver's early life and an account of his medical training. The flashback also covers the years in which Dick meets Nicole, takes her as his patient, and marries her. Fitzgerald believed that this flashback, appearing midway in the novel, had confused his readers. In the revised version he proposed to move material from the middle section to the beginning of the novel and to rearrange the text into five books instead of three. *Tender Is the Night,* reordered, would proceed in a conventionally chronological fashion.

Fitzgerald's plan to republish *Tender Is the Night* came to nothing during his lifetime. He was unable to interest Scribner's or the Modern Library, a reprint house, in publishing a new version and so turned to other projects. He did, however, leave behind a copy of the first edition into which he had marked cuts and emendations that he thought might accomplish his proposed restructuring. This copy of *Tender Is the Night* is preserved among his papers at Princeton University Library. Fitzgerald's penciled markings extend in detail only through the first two chapters of *Tender Is the Night,* suggesting that, as he worked, he came to recognize the impracticability of the idea and abandoned his efforts. It is also possible, of course, that when neither Scribner's nor the Modern Library seemed interested in a reordered text, Fitzgerald put the project on hold but still believed in the efficacy of his plan and would have pursued it, had he lived longer.

In the late 1940s Malcolm Cowley, a prominent critic and editor, received permission from Fitzgerald's literary estate and from Scribner's to put together an edition of the author's "final version." Working from Fitzgerald's marked copy, Cowley published his text in November 1951. Reactions were lukewarm, though the reviews did bring to light some interesting questions about postpublication revision and the reediting of literary works after an author's death.[3] Scribner's kept both texts of *Tender Is the Night* in print into the 1960s, but the Cowley version never gained acceptance among readers, teachers, or critics.

So far as the Cambridge Edition is concerned, the 1951 Cowley text is not an issue. Almost no one in Fitzgerald studies uses this text as a basis for critical interpretation, and it is not in print in the United States.[4] The Cambridge edition of *Tender Is the Night* will follow the 1934 ordering of the text. Fitzgerald's desire to publish his novel with a rearranged chronology is of interest to students of his life and career, but the consensus is that he did not anticipate the near impossibility of taking a text that had been composed with one structure in mind and shifting its parts about to create a radically different structure.[5] It could be argued that the Cambridge Edition should publish both texts, in separate volumes, but this would require heavy emendation of the reordered version and would still not produce a satisfactory text. Fitzgerald did not carry forward his revising far enough to give adequate guidance to an editor. The Cowley edition is a commendable effort, as good a text as Fitzgerald scholars and critics need. The Fitzgerald Trust, which makes decisions about the author's literary estate, has chosen the 1934 text as the one that should be represented in the Cambridge Edition. I concur in that decision.

Let us turn now to the internal chronology of the 1934 text. At issue is the time span covered by the novel. Does *Tender Is the Night* occupy four years, from 1925 to 1929, or five years, from 1925 to 1930? Fitzgerald gives us little help here. Neither "1929" nor "1930" appears as a fixed date in the final scenes of the novel. The year in which the narrative ends must be inferred from the chapters that come before. This, one suspects, was deliberate on Fitzgerald's part—an effort by him not to be heavy-handed in applying one of the morals of his tale. The late Matthew J. Bruccoli, for many years an active and visible scholar in the Fitzgerald field, was the chief proponent of the 1929 ending. In a 1963 monograph called *The Composition of "Tender Is the Night,"* Bruccoli argued that the text should be made to end in 1929. In 1964 he published a list of emendations designed to correct the demonstrable errors in the 1934 text and change its time scheme. He included this same list of emendations, slightly expanded, in a sourcebook entitled *Reader's Companion to F. Scott Fitzgerald's "Tender Is the Night,"* published in 1996.[6]

In all of these publications Bruccoli insisted that *Tender is the Night* should end in 1929. Evidence exists to back up the assertion. When Fitzgerald wrote out his working notes for the novel, likely in August 1932, he *did* mean for the last scene on the Riviera to occur in July 1929. This is beyond question: the notes survive at Princeton and are reproduced on pages 76–82 of *Composition* and pages 5–21 of *Companion.* Twice in these notes Fitzgerald specifies that the novel will conclude in July 1929. Bruccoli's belief is that, in the rush to publish in the spring of 1934, Fitzgerald became confused and introduced errors into the chronology. According to Bruccoli these errors "obscure the time-scheme of the novel and seriously undermine the impact of Book III" (*Composition*, 214).

Bruccoli was disagreeing here with Cowley, who in his 1951 text had permitted the narrative to end in 1930. Bruccoli's conclusions were based also on a remark by the handsome mercenary Tommy Barban to Dick near the end of the 1934 text. Dick asks, "Are you rich, Tommy?" And Tommy, whose command of English is imperfect, answers: "Not as things go now. I got tired of the brokerage business and went away. But I have good stocks in the hands of friends who are holding it for me. All goes well" (353). Bruccoli writes, "Surely this remark belongs to 1929, not 1930" (*Composition*, 215). Bruccoli argues therefore that the chronology of *Tender Is the Night* should be emended to make the narrative end in 1929. "The unexpressed idea," he writes, is "that the new breed of the new-rich Riviera people have less than four months of paper profits left" (*Composition*, 214). Dick's papal blessing to the crowd on the beach, three pages from the end of the 1934 text, therefore becomes highly ironic. These people, who have used him and cast him aside, are on the brink of financial ruin. Their careless way of life will not endure; they will be punished. This is a strong interpretive point and a persuasive reason to make the novel end in July 1929.

The problem is that if one goes by the evidence of the published novel, and of the surviving typescripts and proofs that precede it (as opposed to the 1932 notes, written before most of the novel was composed), it is obvious that the novel ends in 1930.[7] There is no confusion in the surviving typescripts, no altered months or years, and no confusion in the serial text. In 1936 Fitzgerald even inscribed a copy of the first edition to his typist as follows: "F. Scott Fitzgerald requests the pleasure of Laura Guthrie's company in Europe 1917–1930"—an inscription that Bruccoli, to his credit, reproduces on page 188 of the *Companion*. It is likely that, as Fitzgerald composed *Tender Is the Night*, he added a year to its internal chronology in order to accommodate extra material and new scenes that he did not anticipate in his 1932 working notes. In so doing he made another improvement: he extended Dick's period of disintegration by a year, making his fall seem less precipitate and more believable.

If the novel ends in July 1930, Fitzgerald will be making a different point, perhaps a stronger one. The lesson now is that the wealthy Riviera pleasure-seekers are largely immune to the downturn in the American economy. The rich never have to pay the tab. If they, like Tommy Barban, have reliable people handling their assets, then they have retrenched and are riding out the financial panic. Only foolish investors put everything into the stock market during the boom period. More experienced people maintained diversified holdings, with risk minimized. The economy would recover as it always had; in the meantime the very wealthy would go on living their lives without great inconvenience or punishment. This is the insight one takes from *Tender Is the Night* if the novel is permitted to end in 1930. It too is a strong and persuasive point.[8]

Bruccoli carried out his plan to make *Tender Is the Night* end in 1929 in an edition of the novel published by Everyman in London in 1996. This edition was issued during a period when copyright on the novel had lapsed in the United Kingdom. Some 172 emendations were introduced into the Everyman text by Bruccoli, twenty-one of them involving internal chronology. These emendations—in months, years, and ages of characters—were necessary to make the novel end in July 1929.

It is much simpler to allow *Tender Is the Night* to end in July 1930. Emendations on only two pages in the 1934 text will set the time scheme right. The chronology of Dick Diver's life, established from the published text of the novel, sets the pattern. He is born in the spring of 1890. He attends Yale, wins a Rhodes Scholarship, studies at Oxford, and comes back to America to take a medical degree from Johns Hopkins in 1916, at the age of twenty-six. He travels to Vienna to continue his studies; when the United States enters World War I in the spring of 1917, Dick relocates to neutral Switzerland and finishes his postgraduate degree. He joins the American armed forces toward the end of the war and serves in a neurological unit. He meets Nicole Warren in 1918. She is a child of great wealth, the daughter of the industrialist Devereux Warren. Dick takes Nicole as his patient and marries her in the fall of 1919. Six years pass, during which Dick and Nicole have two children and Nicole suffers additional mental breakdowns. Dick rebuilds her personality after each of these relapses, but at a cost to his own health and resilience.

The summer of 1925 finds the Diver family at Gauss's Hotel on the Riviera, where, in the opening scenes of the 1934 text, they meet the young movie actress Rosemary Hoyt. The Divers and their friends move on to Paris in late June; Rosemary and her mother come to the city with them. Dick and Rosemary have a flirtation in Paris but do not become lovers. She returns to Hollywood in July, and the Divers lose touch with her. Dick decides to enter a partnership with Franz Gregorovious in a Swiss psychiatric clinic in December 1925. Dick persuades Baby Warren, Nicole's sister, to allow some of the Warren money to be invested in the clinic. During the years 1926 and 1927 the Divers live away from the clinic while Franz supervises its renovation. By 1928 Dick, Nicole, and their two children are established there, and Dick is treating patients. In the summer of 1928 Nicole has another relapse and deliberately causes their automobile to crash, endangering the lives of Dick, their children, and herself. This is a pivotal incident. Dick's attitude toward Nicole changes; he begins to resent his dual role as husband and therapist and to see that, vampire-like, she is draining him of his energy and vitality.

In November 1928 Dick makes a trip to Rome and encounters Rosemary there. They renew and finally consummate their romance. In May 1929 Franz begins to edge Dick out of the clinic—for alcoholism and other unprofessional behavior. The Divers travel for several months, then return to the Villa Diana, their home on the Riviera, in February 1930. Tommy Barban comes in April 1930; he and Nicole begin their affair in June; Nicole and Dick agree to a divorce in July. Dick, who has recently turned forty, leaves the Riviera in late July 1930.[9]

This is a reasonably complicated chronology. It is remarkable that Fitzgerald made no more errors in constructing it than he did. Five emendations on two pages of the 1934 first edition, 271 and 276, will set the time scheme right.

At 271.7 and 271.14, Fitzgerald indicates that it has been "four years" since the summer of 1925. The passage is set in November 1928; it has therefore been three years and four months since the events of June and July 1925. If both readings are emended to "three years," they will be congruent with a reference five pages on, at 276.22, to a period of "three years" during which Dick has been "the ideal by which Rosemary measured other men." These passages are close enough to each other that they should match. And at 271.15 the following sentence occurs: "Eighteen might look at thirty-four through a rising mist of adolescence; but twenty-two would see thirty-eight with discerning clarity." The first and last of these ages for Rosemary and Dick are correct. She was eighteen when they met; he is thirty-eight at this point in the novel. But the second and third ages are off by one year and should read "thirty-five" and "twenty-one." Also off by one year is Rosemary's age at 276.12. Like the passage on page 271, this one occurs in November 1928; Rosemary should be "twenty-one," not "twenty-two."

Three other readings in the 1934 text are inconsistent with the internal chronology of the novel but do not involve the year in which the novel ends. At 167.6 Nicole's father, Devereaux Warren, tells a therapist named Dr. Dohmler that "Nicole's mother died when she was eleven." This statement contradicts Nicole's recollection, some seventy pages earlier, that "Mother and Baby and I once spent a winter" in Paris "when I was twelve" (89.10). If "twelve" is emended to "ten," the internal chronology will mesh. And at 331.11 the ages of the two Diver children are given as "eleven and nine." At this point Dick and Nicole have not yet been married for ten years. Emendation to "nine and seven" removes the problem on page 331, and a correction from "She was nine" to "She was seven" at 332.13 completes the repair.

Does the internal chronology of the 1934 text need to be emended at all? Unless obvious or radical discrepancies present themselves, even the closest readers of literary texts do not usually keep track of the passing of months, years, seasons, or the ages of characters. Most readers notice such problems only when there are obvious errors or inconsistencies in a single scene or within a few pages of each other, as with pages 271 and 276 of *Tender Is the Night*. In such cases the mistakes can be distracting and do require editorial attention. Even after discovering irregularities such as these, a scholarly editor of a historical bent might elect not to adjust the chronology, thinking of *Tender Is the Night* as a socially constructed text or a sacrosanct "national scripture."[10] Such an editor might call attention to the errors but would not emend the text. This is a defensible stance, applicable to a facsimile edition of a single text or to a diplomatic resetting of an existing version but not to a freshly typeset eclectic edition, such as those being published in the Cambridge series.[11]

Fitzgerald was usually reliable on matters of internal chronology. In the ten volumes of his writing that I have edited so far for the Cambridge Edition, I have discovered only five works of fiction in which the chronology is clearly off. I have introduced emendations into only one of these texts; the other four I have left unchanged. The texts are *This Side of Paradise* (1920), *The Beautiful and Damned* (1922), "Winter Dreams" (1922), "A Nice Quiet Place" (1930), and *Trimalchio*, which was not published until 2000. A description of the problems in these texts will give additional background to this discussion of *Tender Is the Night*.

In his first novel, *This Side of Paradise*, Fitzgerald makes four errors in chronology. He places a football game in the wrong month, adds a year to a recollection, misdates a letter, and drops a month from the duration of a love affair. It's not a surprise to find such errors: *This Side of Paradise* is a crowded, episodic novel, patched together in the summer of 1919 from numerous pieces of fiction, poetry, and drama that Fitzgerald had composed over the previous two-year period.[12] All four problems can be repaired by simple emendations. These changes have no effect on style, narration, symbolism, characterization, or imagery. For the Cambridge text of *This Side of Paradise*, I changed "October" to "November" at 36.25, "two years" to "a year" at 141.5, "March" to "January" at 152.23, and "two months" to "three months" at 178.16.[13]

It is not so easy with Fitzgerald's second novel, *The Beautiful and Damned*. In the first-edition text of 1922 Fitzgerald gives three different birthdays to his heroine, Gloria Gilbert. At 192.23 we are told that she will be "twenty-four in August." At 276.7 she is about to turn "twenty-six in May." And near the end of the novel, at 391.29, 393.13, and 393.23, we read that she will be "twenty-nine in February." These passages are far enough apart that most readers do not notice the three birthdays—though Zelda, on whom the character of Gloria was based, caught the inconsistencies. In a spoof review of *The Beautiful and Damned* entitled "Friend Husband's Latest," she noted the problem but got one of the months wrong: "I regret to remark that on finishing the book I feel no confidence as to [Gloria's] age," wrote Zelda. "Her birthday is in one place given as occurring in February and in another place May and in the third place in September."[14]

It is impossible to establish a single month of birth for Gloria. If one fixes upon February, for example, one must tinker with other readings more than is normally acceptable in a scholarly text. On page 192 of the first edition one finds this sentence: "But Gloria—she would be twenty-four in August and was in an attractive but sincere panic about it. Six years to thirty!" This is a typical reference to Gloria's birthday; she dreads the passage of time, knowing that eventually she will lose her freshness and beauty. If her birthday is repositioned throughout the novel to February, then a great many other emendations will be required. In the passage just quoted, for example, "twenty-four" will have to become "twenty-five"; "August" will need to be changed to "February"; and "Six" will have to be altered to "Five." The passage occurs in a scene set in the spring of 1915. If Gloria's birthday is shifted backward from August to February of that year, then she will have only recently turned twenty-five and will have nine or ten months until another birthday occurs—too far in the future for her to be fretful about. Similar problems pop up if one chooses August or May as the month of birth. An emendation in one spot requires another and another until the chronology of the entire novel is in disarray. For the Cambridge text, I left the birthdays alone and only commented on the matter in the introduction.[15]

The chronology of Fitzgerald's superb 1922 short story "Winter Dreams," often taught as a preliminary treatment of the themes of *The Great Gatsby*, is slightly skewed. The single date mentioned in the narrative is February 1917—at the end of section V of the story, just before the protagonist, Dexter Green, enters World War I. But by working backward through the period preceding the war, one discovers that Fitzgerald has lost track of the year 1906–7. Dexter's age, given earlier in section IV as twenty-five, should be twenty-six.[16] It would be easy enough to make the emendation, but there is a subtle difference between the ages of twenty-five and twenty-six, especially for Dexter, who at this point is about to change his life by abandoning his pursuit of social status among the bourgeoisie of Minnesota. He will leave the Midwest and seek success on Wall Street. The error in chronology is not bothersome to a reader; I therefore made no emendation and, for the Cambridge text, only mentioned the problem in an explanatory note.[17]

"A Nice Quiet Place," a story in the Josephine Perry series of 1930–31, contains an error in its time scheme that, like the flaw in "Winter Dreams," is resistant to emendation. In "A Nice Quiet Place," Josephine is compelled by her parents to spend the greater part of one summer at a small resort in northern Michigan. Though she is only fifteen years old, Josephine has already developed a reputation as a "speed" in her hometown of Lake Forest, Illinois, a suburb for the wealthy situated some thirty miles north of Chicago.

Josephine's parents want to take her out of circulation for a period in hopes that the swimming and fishing at "Island Farms," as the resort is called, will distract her from the social whirl in Lake Forest. Josephine is furious but has no choice. She does, however, extract one concession from her mother: she will be allowed to return home in time for a house party to be given by Ed Bement, a member of her social circle. We are told on the third page of the story (p. 207 in the Cambridge text) that Ed's party is to take place "the first of September."

Problems with the internal chronology of the story manifest themselves twelve pages later. Josephine's older sister Constance, who envies Josephine's success with boys, is to be married in mid-August. Josephine suspects that Constance was behind her rustication to Island Farms and wants revenge. She gets it (on page 219) at Ed Bement's party, which has unaccountably been moved to an earlier point, in the first week of August, so that it can precede the wedding Josephine means to spoil.

An editor might fix things by changing the date of the party early in the story or postponing the date of the wedding later on, but the first repair makes Josephine's stay at Island Farms too short to accommodate the machinations of the plot that must occur there, and the second puts Constance's wedding hard up against the beginning of the academic year, when Josephine and her friends must leave Lake Forest for the eastern prep schools they attend. Some experimental fiddling with the text produces a predictable result: one emendation necessitates another; this triggers a third and fourth until the chronology of the entire story unravels. My decision was not to emend. The two dates for Ed's party are twelve pages apart; those pages are full of distractions, so many that only the most detail-obsessed reader would notice the problem with internal chronology. I called attention to the inconsistency in dates with a note on page 329 of the apparatus and left it at that.

One final example comes from *Trimalchio,* the penultimate version of *The Great Gatsby* that appeared as a separate volume in the Cambridge Edition in 2000. This text, submitted for publication by Fitzgerald to Scribner's in October 1924, is preserved in the set of galley proofs that he revised extensively to produce *The Great Gatsby.* These galleys are among his papers at Princeton.[18] Early in the first chapter of both *Trimalchio* and *The Great Gatsby,* Daisy Buchanan says to her cousin, Nick Carraway, "You ought to see the baby." Two lines later Daisy adds, "She's asleep. She's three years old."[19] The chronology of the narrative indicates that the child should be two. She was born in April 1920, ten months after Daisy married Tom Buchanan. The scene in which

Daisy mentions her daughter's age occurs in June 1922. An emendation from "three" to "two" is probably called for, but when I published the Cambridge edition of *Trimalchio,* I only pointed out the problem in a textual note (162). Because *Trimalchio* was the penultimate version of *The Great Gatsby,* never brought fully into publishable shape by Fitzgerald, I left the reading alone. If this had been an edition of *The Great Gatsby,* however, I would probably have made the emendation.

Emending the chronology of a work of fiction is tricky. It is probably impossible to be consistent in editorial strategy, even within the oeuvre of a single author. For Fitzgerald's writings, the routine emendations are easy. It is simple enough always to preserve his holograph spelling "equeal" in texts of his letters but to correct to "equal" in stories, essays, and novels. It is easy to regularize to "grey" and "theatre," British spellings that he always used in his handwritten drafts. And it is beyond argument that one should make a character's hair color the same in a novel where it is auburn throughout the text except for one page, where it is blond.[20] Beyond this sort of emending, however, things get murky.

All scholarly editors look for emendations that will "sell" their editions. Their fellow editors, and perhaps a few specialists who concentrate on the author, will recognize the value of a full-dress edition, with its history of composition, tables of emendation, explanatory notes, illustrations, and appendixes. These readers will not require spectacular emendations. Nonspecialists, however, will question the purpose of so much labor if the text itself is not changed in a dramatic way. This causes editors to overreach, to insist too vigorously on the importance of the emendations they do make or to invent textual cruxes which (they assert) must be resolved if the work is to be correctly understood. One sympathizes. It is not always easy to explain what one does as a scholarly editor or why one does it. The temptation is to overstate.

The most important factors in making editorial decisions about chronology are whether the errors are distracting to readers and whether emendations can be introduced (simple ones, and only a few of them) without making other emendations necessary. This, one assumes, is what any author would want in an edition of his or her writing, though an author's intentions are impossible finally to know with certainty. In the case of *Tender Is the Night,* the mistakes in the chronology of the 1934 text are not particularly bothersome, but they are apparent to anyone who pays attention to the time scheme of the book. Emendation of the passages discussed above will bring the chronology of the 1934 text into internal alignment. Fitzgerald's language will be only slightly altered; characterization and connotation will be changed only a little. *Tender Is the Night,* in the Cambridge series, will end in July 1930, as the preponderance of internal and external evidence indicates.

NOTES

1. James L. W. West III, *"Tender Is the Night,* 'Jazzmania,' and the Ellingson Matricide," in *Twenty-First-Century Readings of "Tender Is the Night,"* ed. William Blazek and Laura Rattray (Liverpool: Liverpool University Press, 2007), 34–49.

2. The best chapter-length account of the making of the novel is Scott Donaldson's "A Short History of *Tender Is the Night,"* in his collection *Fitzgerald and Hemingway: Works and Days* (New York: Columbia University Press, 2009), 119–46. An earlier version of this piece appeared in *Writing the American Classics,* ed. James Barbour and Tom Quirk (Chapel Hill: University of North Carolina Press, 1990), 177–208.

3. See, for example, John Chamberlain, "A Reviewer's Notebook," *Freeman* 2 (19 November 1951): 121–22; Arthur Mizener, "An Author's Final Version," *Saturday Review of Literature* 34 (8 December 1951): 19; Charles Poore, "Books of The Times," *New York Times,* 15 November 1951, 27; and Budd Schulberg, "Prodded by Pride and Desperation," *New York Times Book Review,* 18 November 1951, 5, 38.

4. For an argument in favor of the 1951 text, see Milton Stern, *"Tender Is the Night:* The Text Itself," in *Critical Essays on F. Scott Fitzgerald's "Tender Is the Night"* (Boston: G. K. Hall, 1986), 21–31.

5. On the shortcomings of the reordered text, see Brian Higgins and Hershel Parker, "Sober Second Thoughts: Fitzgerald's 'Final Version' of *Tender Is the Night,"* *Proof* 4 (1975): 129–52.

6. Matthew J. Bruccoli, *The Composition of "Tender Is the Night": A Study of the Manuscripts* (Pittsburgh: University of Pittsburgh Press, 1963); Bruccoli, "Material for a Centenary Edition of *Tender Is the Night,"* *Studies in Bibliography* 17 (1964): 177–93; Bruccoli, *Reader's Companion to F. Scott Fitzgerald's "Tender Is the Night"* (Columbia: University of South Carolina Press, 1996).

7. The manuscripts and typescripts of *Tender Is the Night* are among Fitzgerald's papers at Princeton, together with proofs and correspondence in the Scribner's archive there. Most of the drafts have been reproduced in facsimile in *F. Scott Fitzgerald Manuscripts,* 16 vols., ed. Matthew J. Bruccoli (New York: Garland, 1991).

8. This interpretation fits in with Fitzgerald's concept of "emotional bankruptcy." Dick has foolishly and impulsively invested all his personal resources—his talent, intellect, and love—in Nicole. She has turned out to be a poor investment, draining him of his energy and emotion and paying nothing back. By the end of the novel Dick finds himself incapable of replenishment, emotionally bankrupt.

9. I wish to acknowledge the considerable assistance of Gregg Baptista, my research assistant in 2008–9, in establishing this chronology.

10. This is Jerome J. McGann's term, used throughout *A Critique of Modern Textual Criticism.*

11. For a statement of the governing editorial principles of the Cambridge Edition, see the introduction to *This Side of Paradise,* ed. James L. W. West III (Cambridge: Cambridge University Press, 1995), xl–xlii.

12. James L. W. West III, *The Making of "This Side of Paradise"* (Philadelphia: University of Pennsylvania Press, 1983).

13. For details, see appendix 2, "Chronology and Characters," in the Cambridge edition of *This Side of Paradise,* 396–400.

14. The review appeared in the *New York Tribune,* 2 April 1922; it has been reprinted in *Zelda Fitzgerald: The Collected Writings,* ed. Matthew J. Bruccoli (New York: Scribner's, 1991), 388.

15. F. Scott Fitzgerald, *The Beautiful and Damned,* ed. James L. W. West III (Cambridge: Cambridge University Press, 2008), xxvii.

16. "Winter Dreams" was first published in the December 1922 issue of *Metropolitan Magazine.* Fitzgerald revised the story and collected it in *All the Sad Young Men* (New York: Scribner's, 1923).

This revised text is included in F. Scott Fitzgerald, *All the Sad Young Men,* ed. James L. W. West III (Cambridge: Cambridge University Press, 2007).

17.  The explanatory note is published on p. 466 of the Cambridge *All the Sad Young Men.* Dexter's age appears on p. 78 of the Scribner's first edition and p. 58 of the Cambridge text. A similar argument about the connotations of particular ages might be applied to *Tender Is the Night.* The majority of the emendations discussed above have to do with the ages of characters.

18.  For a short history of the making of the novel, see James L. W. West III, "The Composition and Publication of *The Great Gatsby,*" in *Approaches to Teaching Fitzgerald's "The Great Gatsby,"* ed. Jackson R. Bryer and Nancy P. VanArsdale (New York: Modern Language Association, 2009), 19–24.

19.  *Trimalchio: An Early Version of "The Great Gatsby,"* ed. James L. W. West III (Cambridge: Cambridge University Press, 2000), 12. A loose-leaf, boxed facsimile of an unrevised set of galleys, identical in typeset text to the galleys at Princeton, was published by Bruccoli as *Trimalchio* (Columbia: University of South Carolina Press, 2000). This set of galleys is part of the Bruccoli collection at the Thomas Cooper Library, University of South Carolina.

20.  This happened when Fitzgerald incorporated the typescript of a short story about a character named Stephen Palms, who is blond, into the manuscript of *This Side of Paradise,* the protagonist of which is the auburn-haired Amory Blaine. See p. 208 of the Cambridge edition of *This Side of Paradise* and the emendation note on pp. 281–82. In one of the Basil Duke Lee stories, Basil's hair is black and brown within a single story—"The Scandal Detectives" (1928). An emendation from "brown-haired" to "black-haired" fixes the problem. In the Josephine Perry stories, mentioned earlier in this essay, Josephine's eyes are three different colors: green, brown, and "grey" (Fitzgerald preferred the British spelling). I settled on "grey" because it was the color used most frequently by Fitzgerald in the stories. See the apparatus of *The Basil, Josephine, and Gwen Stories,* pp. 326 and 330, emendations entries for 18.11–12, 226.7, and 250.22. But in Dreiser's *Jennie Gerhardt,* the subject of a chapter earlier in this collection, I did not regularize eye color. Jennie's eyes are blue in chapter 1 but gray in chapters 58 and 59. Her blue eyes, early in the novel, suggest her openness and innocence; her gray eyes later on, after she has endured much personal sadness, betoken her melancholy. Because the inconsistencies are almost four hundred pages apart, I did not emend. See the Pennsylvania edition of the novel, pp. 8, 396, and 409 of the text and p. 490 of the textual commentary.

# ANNOTATING MR. FITZGERALD

Anyone who has written historical notes for a scholarly edition has learned to spot "glossable" references in mid- to late twentieth-century texts. Most readers of J. D. Salinger's *The Catcher in the Rye* (1951), for example, now need to be told who the Broadway stars Alfred Lunt and Lynn Fontanne were. Philip Roth's *Zuckerman Unbound* (1981) probably already requires annotations about the quiz show scandals of the 1950s and about Charles Van Doren and Herbert Stempel, contestants whose lives were ruined by the disclosures. Don DeLillo's *Underworld* (1997) will soon need a description of Truman Capote's Black and White Ball, along with some information about J. Edgar Hoover's cross-dressing and his relationship with Clyde Tolson. And future readers of Bret Easton Ellis's novel *Glamorama* (1999), should anyone still be reading Ellis fifty years from now, will require a flock of footnotes to identify the multitudinous quasi-celebrities whose names appear in the narrative. The Broadway actors and public exposés and glitter events and minor celebs that turn up in these narratives will all have been forgotten, or will be so imprecisely remembered as to need annotation.

That's the position I find myself in as the editor and annotator of the Cambridge edition of F. Scott Fitzgerald's writings. His narratives are packed with references to contemporary politicians, sports figures, theater impresarios, movie queens, criminals, monarchs, and war heroes, not to mention restaurants and cabarets in New York of the 1920s, plus museums and cathedrals and bistros and people of interest in Europe of that decade. His works are also peppered with the names of writers, serious and popular, and with titles and quotations from their stories and poems.

He knew where everything was at Princeton, and in his early writings he frequently moved his characters across that campus. He set other early fiction in central Manhattan of the teens and twenties. His characters go to Tiffany's and Brooks Brothers, Delmonico's and the Yale Club, the Vanderbilt and the Plaza and the Waldorf-Astoria, and to a great many other places that have long since vanished from the New York scene. And toward the middle of his career he set some of his best short stories in his home town of St. Paul, Minnesota, as it had existed during his adolescent years, from about 1908 to 1913.

The humble editor is thus presented with some problems. How much of this needs to be identified and explained? For whom should it be glossed? How thoroughly should it be annotated? Does one engage in interpretation, pointing out how references and allusions function in the stories, or does one give just the facts? Deciding what and for whom and how much to annotate causes some serious head-scratching.

First, how much needs to be identified? How much do people really need to know? For example, do readers need to be told about the chariot-race sign on Broadway, mentioned in chapter 1 of *This Side of Paradise*? It's safe to say that people who read the novel today have no idea what this sign was. Most of these people, all the same, probably read the novel with normal comprehension, understanding the major themes, characters, and motives. Perhaps they don't really need to know about the chariot-race sign. But the reference does matter, and learning what Fitzgerald had in mind when he used it does add something to one's understanding of the story. Amory Blaine, the protagonist of *This Side of Paradise*, sees the sign during a trip to New York City during his first year at St. Regis', an eastern prep school at which he is unhappy. He has been targeted by his fellow students for his vanity and self-absorption, and he is a pariah. Amory goes to the city in February to see George M. Cohan and Lila Rhodes in *The Little Millionaire*, a rags-to-riches musical on Broadway. Amory has been in New York before, but always during the day. "This time he saw it by electric light," the narrator tells us, "and romance gleamed from the chariot-race sign on Broadway and from the women's eyes at the Astor."[1]

One understands about the women's eyes at the Astor, but why should "romance gleam" from a sign? What was special about this particular sign? Some digging reveals that the chariot-race sign was the largest and most famous of the newfangled electric signs then being erected in Manhattan. It sat atop the Hotel Normandie at Thirty-Eighth and Broadway, overlooking Herald Square. Inspired by General Lew Wallace's bestselling 1880 novel *Ben-Hur*, the apparatus was formally titled "The Fiery Chariot Race in New York." Measuring sixty by ninety feet, it depicted the famous race from the novel, with horses and chariots and charioteers speeding around an arena at a furious gallop—an illusion created by rapidly flashing colored lights. Dust rose from beneath the horses' hoofs, and flames belched from braziers at either side, giving a lurid glow to the surrounding area on Broadway. At night there was almost always a crowd of tourists at the spot, gawking up at the bright tableau. It was written about in newspapers and magazines; journalists were fond of noting details about its workings. It employed some 20,000 lightbulbs that flashed 2,500 times a minute; it contained 70,000 electrical connections and half a million feet of wire. But "The Fiery Chariot Race in New York" did more than entertain tourists: it was first and foremost an advertising vehicle. One could rent time on the sign, which flashed out a series of advertising slogans along its top, the whole sequence of ads taking about ten minutes from start to finish. Thus as spectators watched the chariots and charioteers, they were urged to buy this or that variety of toothpaste or hair oil, or a popular brand of auto tire or perfume or underwear.

I had fun collecting this information. I even found several photographs of the sign at the New-York Historical Society. The sign was a predecessor of the Camel cigarette sign on Times Square during the early 1960s (it blew smoke rings—remember?) and of the enormous Calvin Klein billboards there in more recent decades. But does the chariot-race sign have any significance in Fitzgerald's novel? Here are some possible applications: When Amory sees it, he is miserable at St. Regis' and has come to the city for escape. The huge, flashing sign must epitomize for him the glamour of New York, which both soothes and energizes him. New York is a city that he decides, then and there, to make his mark on. And it's significant that a few years later he'll try to score his first success as a writer of advertising slogans, exactly the sort of verbiage that's flashing across the top of the sign. Amory's first and only employment in the novel is writing jingles at an ad agency. He fails at that job and as a consequence loses Rosalind Connage, the young woman he adores. She chooses wealth and social position over love, marrying a rich boy named Dawson Rider. This is the first statement in all of Fitzgerald's writings of one of his great themes: the authority of money, its power to subvert love and human feeling. Because Amory has little money and cannot sell himself in the ad game, he cannot win the golden girl. What better symbol of commerce, early in the novel, than a looming, glittering, electric advertising sign on Broadway, paired in Fitzgerald's sentence with the alluring eyes of the women at the Hotel Astor?

Perhaps it's also important that the chariot-race sign took its inspiration from a successful novel, *Ben-Hur,* since Amory has ambitions to be a writer. In fact, Amory's creator, F. Scott Fitzgerald, sitting in the attic of his parents' home in St. Paul and inscribing these words on his manuscript sheet, was try-ing to make *his* mark by writing a novel that would (and, in fact, did) enjoy a run on the bestseller lists, just as *Ben-Hur* had. And finally, for people who savor coincidences, it's interesting that Fitzgerald would later, while in Europe in the mid-1920s, become friendly with the screen star Carmel Myers and with other movie people in Rome who were filming the first version of *Ben-Hur*. He visited the movie set several times and used material from those visits in *Tender Is the Night*.

One can spin out the possible significance of one of these annotations to considerable length, but how much of this should be printed in a scholarly edition? How much will Cambridge University Press allow, or the reader need? If one has dug up the information, then the temptation is strong to put it all in—and to interpret it. My decision for the early volumes in the Cambridge Edition was to stick pretty much to the facts, giving details about the chariot-race sign but not mentioning Amory's job as a writer of ad copy or Fitzgerald's visits to the *Ben-Hur* movie set, nor did I attempt in the annotation to present the chariot-race sign as a symbol of anything. However, as I've prepared notes for the later volumes, I've slipped in a few hints about how a reference might illuminate a passage. One must be careful not to explicate too much, not to cue the reader too insistently, but a little guidance can be helpful.

How much can the editor assume that readers will know? It all depends on who those readers are envisioned as being. Is one annotating only for Fitzger-ald specialists and people with doctorates in American literature? Surely not: Fitzgerald has a great many readers outside academe. Should the audience be thought of as American readers only or British readers as well? It makes a difference. Is the base audience teachers and academics, or graduate students, or undergraduates? Or is one annotating for educated lay readers or, more broadly, for people all over the world who are interested in Fitzgerald's work? The answer is that one is annotating for all of these audiences simultaneously, and not least for the international readers, since Fitzgerald has quite large fol-lowings in Europe, Asia, and elsewhere.

However, editors who address annotations to large audiences end up including rather many notes and identifications. This can get you in trouble with reviewers who want something to carp about and who fix on the issue of over-annotation. If you push the boundaries and include, for example, a note identifying Woodrow Wilson, then you risk the ire of the reviewer who says, "Good lord, *everyone* knows who Woodrow Wilson was!" The truth, though, is that everyone doesn't. An informal questionnaire administered to some bright graduate students in American literature a few years ago revealed that all of them knew Wilson to have been a president of the United States, but less than half knew when he had been president, and none knew that he had been president of Princeton before he was president of the United States—which, of course, was what interested Fitzgerald. And there are surely many readers in Italy or Japan or India (significant markets for these Fitzgerald editions) who know even less about the twenty-eighth president of the United States. Therefore, I glossed Woodrow Wilson and ducked.

Some editors become genuinely irritated by complaints about over-annotation, and they strike back. One editor friend of mine, weary of grousing from British reviewers that he was annotating too much, included the following identification for a reference by his author: "Jesus Christ: Son of God; born Bethlehem, B.C. 00; died Jerusalem, A.D. 33." When challenged, my friend replied quite blandly that many of his poet's contemporary readers were Muslims or Buddhists and that they needed the help.

One must also consider the shelf life of these editions. One hopes that they will last for a long time, that they will reside in library stacks for at least the next century, and that they will endure even longer in digital form. One must therefore think ahead. How many readers in 2099 will be able to identify Woodrow Wilson, much less the chariot-race sign on Broadway? Not many.

Fitzgerald liked to make lists. Here's one I made of references in his writings that need glossing. How many people today can identify Three-Finger Brown (a pitcher for the Cubs), Robert Hugh Benson (a Catholic apologist), Edward Carpenter (a British reformer), Ralph Adams Cram (the architect whose firm designed the collegiate Gothic buildings on the Princeton campus), Donald Hankey (a British soldier/author from World War I), Daniel Florence Cohalan (an American judge who favored revolution by the Irish), Lady Diana Manners (an English beauty used as a model by Evelyn Waugh and Nancy Mitford), Gaby Deslys (a dancer known for her jewel collection and her romantic connections with royalty), or Anna Held (a headliner in the Ziegfeld Follies, famous for her milk baths)? Who were Queen Marie de Medici of France, Queen Margherita di Savoia of Italy, and Queen Marie Alexandra Victoria of Romania (whose portrait was featured in advertisements for Pond's cold cream)? Does anyone remember Paul Nelson, the inventor of the "Maison Suspendue"; Merian Cooper, one of the producers of the first *King Kong* movie; or R. F. Outcault, the creator of the Buster Brown comic strip? How about the wrestler Man Mountain Dean, a professional strong-man who was featured in two films with Jean Harlow, or Pearl White, the

"Lady Daredevil of the Fillums," who starred in the movie serial *The Perils of Pauline*? They're all mentioned in Fitzgerald's essays, stories, and novels. All were part of the daily skin-wash of journalism and celebrity gossip that flowed around and over his readers.

No one today recognizes these lobster palaces and rooftop restaurants from postwar New York: the Midnight Frolic, Devinières, Bistolary's, the Cocoanut Grove (not the one from the 1950s but the one from the 1920s), the Palais Royal, Montmartre, and Sans Souci. Which of those nightspots were upmarket and which were downscale? In which one did Gilda Gray dance the Shimmy? Did she invent the dance, or did Mae West? How, in fact, did one perform the Shimmy? For that matter, how did one do the Castle Walk? (Vernon and Irene Castle, the dance team who invented it, aren't around today to give a demonstration.) Where was Brooks Brothers located in 1914? Where on Fifth Avenue was Tiffany's in 1922? When did the Yale Club move to its present location at Vanderbilt and Forty-Fourth?

Did Stonewall Jackson really suck on lemons during the Battle of Chancellorsville? What was important about the Battle of Château Thierry? What exactly was the False Armistice, and who caused it? When did Prohibition actually go into effect? Were Fatimas a variety of cigarettes or a brand of cookies? What did it mean if you wore a moujik blouse? How did a cut-out muffler work, and what was a motometer? What were Fred Harvey restaurants? What was in bad taste about wearing "an extreme Empire gown" to a small-town dinner party? (Answer: too much décolleté.) What was special about Mae Murray's clothes? About Gloria Swanson's nose? Why was it a mark of high social status to have a Manhattan telephone number with a Rhinelander, Plaza, or Circle exchange? What exactly was a Prince of Wales suit? Was Theda Bara really born in the shadow of the Sphinx, and was her name really a reverse anagram for "Arab Death"?

These things keep me awake at night. Here's another. What were the differences among the Floradora Girl, the Gibson Girl, and the Djer-Kiss Girl? Fitzgerald mentions all three in his writings: all were models of female beauty between 1900 and 1925, but their images were quite different, and Fitzgerald mentions them to imply things about women in his stories.

The Floradora Girls were popular on Broadway early in the new century. They appeared in the British musical *Floradora*, which opened in New York in 1900, and they epitomized the rather buxom ideal of female beauty at the time. The Floradora Girls were six in number; they wore high-collared, frilly dresses and picture hats, and sometimes they carried parasols. At the high point of the show, they would promenade on the stage with six swains in ascots and top hats, the group singing the hit song "Tell Me Pretty Maiden." Women in the sextette often had later successes in the theater or married millionaires; one of the girls in the show, in fact, was Evelyn Nesbit, who snagged Harry K. Thaw, who later shot Stanford White, who had earlier kept Evelyn as his mistress.

The Gibson Girl was different. She was the creation of the illustrator Charles Dana Gibson, whose pen-and-ink drawings of her appeared in *Life* magazine, in albums, on wall posters, and on pillows and scarves. The Gibson girl had upswept hair, aristocratic features, a long neck, and strong shoulders. Often she was pictured in a high-collared shirtwaist and long skirt, with a golf club or tennis racquet in hand. She represented something different from the Floradora Girl: the Gibson Girl was a newer woman, more arch and self-assured, slightly masculinized, confident of her place in society and not much impressed by the young men who pursued her.

The Djer-Kiss Girl was something else again. She appeared in magazine advertisements for Djer-Kiss, a line of perfume and women's toiletries from Kerkoff of Paris. The Djer-Kiss Girl, as drawn by the artist Malaga Grenet, was epicene and nymphlike; usually she was pictured applying cosmetics before a mirror. She was typical of a familiar feminine ideal of the 1920s—trig and boyish, with a flat bustline, bobbed hair, and a well-powdered nose.

Fitzgerald mentioned the Floradora Girl or the Gibson Girl or the Djer-Kiss Girl quite deliberately in his stories and novels. Each mention adds to atmosphere or characterization, and each suggests a period of about eight or ten years during which that girl was a model for female beauty. Fitzgerald must have been confident that his readers would pick up on the references. They would have in the 1920s, but they don't today. That's where the scholarly annotator steps in.

Annotations can give insight into Fitzgerald's memories of songs, stage stars, and Broadway productions. References that must have had particular meaning for him appear over and over in his writings. An example: in the fall of 1911, as a fifteen-year-old prep school student at the Newman School in Hackensack, New Jersey, Fitzgerald made his first trip to New York City and attended his first Broadway musical, *The Quaker Girl.* The title character was played by Ina Claire, a pretty hazel-eyed singer and comedienne who had only recently turned eighteen. She appeared as an English girl who wins the heart of a handsome young American visitor to her rural town. Fitzgerald was starstruck and stagestruck: "From that day forth my desk bulged with

Gilbert & Sullivan librettos and dozens of notebooks containing the germs of dozens of musical comedies," he later wrote.[2] In his short fiction and personal essays he mentioned *The Quaker Girl* repeatedly—for example, in "Who's Who—and Why" (1920), "The Freshest Boy" (1928), "My Lost City" (1933), and "Teamed with Genius" (1940). Some of the references are humorous. Basil Duke Lee, the autobiographical hero of "The Freshest Boy," misspells the title of the play as "The Quacker Girl" in a letter home to his mother; and Pat Hobby, a washed-up Hollywood scriptwriter in "Teamed with Genius," takes a flutter on a filly named Quaker Girl at the Santa Anita racetrack one afternoon. The title of the play had apparently lodged itself in Fitzgerald's mind and popped up from time to time as he sat at his writing desk.

Fitzgerald used the titles of Broadway hit songs to establish the dates of his stories. When the adolescent characters in "That Kind of Party," written in 1928, sing Otto Harbach's "Every Little Movement" and Joseph E. Howard's "I Wonder Who's Kissing Her Now," we know that the year in which the story is set is 1910, when both songs were popular. References to George M. Cohan's "Over There" and Geoffrey O'Hara's "K-K-K-Katy" (the "Sensational Stammering Song Success Sung by the Soldiers and Sailors") signal that a narrative is set during World War I. "Yes, We Have No Bananas!"—mentioned in "How to Live on Practically Nothing a Year" and "Echoes of the Jazz Age"—establishes the date as 1923, when Eddie Cantor was singing the song in his Broadway show *Make It Snappy.*

Where does one find the information for these notes? Anywhere and everywhere. Much is available on the Internet. Encyclopedias and reference books are helpful, but often it's necessary to locate old Baedekers or to find maps and train schedules from ninety years ago. One must travel to libraries—frequently to the New York Public Library (both the main branch at Fifth and Forty-Second and the Library for the Performing Arts at Lincoln Center), or to the Mudd Library at Princeton, where the university archives are kept. One telephones college alumni associations or pages through art books in search of period advertisements. Sometimes one hires researchers on Long Island or in Minnesota to look through historical-society records, or one tracks down sheet music for popular songs of the 1910s and 1920s. And endlessly, it seems, one clicks around in the online edition of the *New York Times.*

Sometimes it feels like donkey work, faintly absurd and a little déclassé. Editors who annotate John Milton, for example, write learned notes about biblical scripture and English history, about the Smectymnian Controversy and the Manichean Heresy. An editor of Fitzgerald, by contrast, must summarize the plot of *Mary Ware, the Little Colonel's Chum* or explain how a detachable collar worked or summarize the rules of double-dummy mah-jongg. There are plenty of intellectually respectable allusions in Fitzgerald: I've written glosses for Heraclitus, Hume, and Bergson; for Samuel Butler, Samuel Pepys, and Samuel Johnson; for Byron, Shelley, and Tennyson; for Renan, Bourget, and Verlaine; for Trotsky and Kerensky; for the two Aaron Burrs, father and son; and for Black Jack Pershing and Light-Horse Harry Lee (a Princeton alum). Almost anyone can write competent notes on these figures. It's a considerable challenge, on the other hand, to gloss a tune like "I Ain't Gonna Give Nobody None o' This Jelly Roll," a 1919 ditty made famous by Sidney Bechet and His New Orleans Feet Warmers. And do I explain the double entendre in the title?

Speaking of double entendre, a good deal of it is created by the changed meanings of words and phrases that Fitzgerald used in the 1920s and 1930s. When he describes a fifteen-year-old charmer as "a veteran of many affairs," he naturally means flirtations. Must the plodding editor explain this? And what about the prom-trotter in Fitzgerald's famous tale "May Day" who, at a Yale alumni dance at Delmonico's, is "kissed once and made love to six times" before midnight? Try to gloss that one without appearing foolish.

There are compensations. Preparing these annotations gives one new respect for Fitzgerald's range of knowledge, which extended from serious literature and philosophy to European and American history to contemporary politics to popular music and dance to the Broadway stage. Some of his allusions in his early works, especially in *This Side of Paradise,* are faked, but he was young when he wrote that book. As he grew older, he read and traveled and became more sophisticated. He turned into a magpie, picking up a great array of knowledge and using it in his fiction. The annotations allow one to track his intellectual progress.

Why perform this labor? What purpose does it serve? One hopes that it helps readers, that it enlarges their understanding of Fitzgerald's novels, stories, and essays. The notes are meant to accomplish what such notes have always been intended to do: help re-create the social and popular milieu of a time, identify literary allusions, explain forgotten manners and mores, and give access to the mind and the times of the writer who created the narratives. Annotations will point scholars and biographers in new directions; they will give critics different things to write about. And they will be helpful to teachers, who can use them to add color and detail to their lectures, or just to show off.

There are important textual cruxes in Fitzgerald's works—the dash at the end of *This Side of Paradise,* for example, or the orgastic/orgiastic variant in

*The Great Gatsby,* or the two versions of *Tender Is the Night*—but speaking generally one doesn't find the kinds of editorial interference or bowdlerization in Fitzgerald that one finds in Dreiser, Faulkner, and Hemingway. It may therefore turn out that the major contribution these Cambridge editions make to the study of Fitzgerald, besides gathering all of his writings in one series, will be to annotate them thoroughly—to re-create, as successfully as such efforts can, the intellectual and social world of the author, Mr. Fitzgerald.

NOTES

1. The Cambridge edition of *This Side of Paradise,* 35.
2. "Who's Who—and Why," in *My Lost City: Personal Essays, 1920–1940* (Cambridge: Cambridge University Press, 2005), 3.

# KEEPER OF THE FLAME

*Editing the Literary Remains of William Styron*

It's a commonplace among scholarly editors that damage is often done to posthumously published texts by keepers of the flame—surviving spouses, children, friends, trade editors, amanuenses, and others charged with the responsibility of preparing a writer's literary remains for print. In many editorial narratives, these flame-tenders are cast as misguided meddlers who have unwisely altered the texts. Acolytes are accused of committing an array of misdemeanors, from misreading the author's hand to bowdlerizing the texts to blunting the force of the writing to masking the names of people who might be offended. Some of the offenses are genuinely serious: keepers of the flame have cut passages to protect themselves, removed complimentary references to their personal rivals, or improved the texts according to their notions of what the author should have written. Most of these desecrators are amateurs, not scholarly editors who are experienced in working with manuscripts, collating texts, emending them, and compiling lists of variants. But what if the editor *is* such a person? Presumably he or she will bring to the task a sensitivity to authorial intention, a desire to fulfill the wishes of the late writer, and a gentle editorial hand.

This is the situation in which I find myself with the literary remains of William Styron. I published a biography of Styron, entitled *William Styron: A Life,* with Random House in 1998, eight years before his death. But I began working on Styron's writings and career in the mid-1970s as his *bibliographer,* long before I thought of writing a biography of anyone. I continued this bibliographical labor throughout the 1980s and 1990s until Styron's death in 2006, keeping track of everything he published. I also worked with his manuscripts, both at the Library of Congress and at Duke University, his alma mater. It therefore fell to me to help with the posthumous publications. If nothing else, I was the person who had all of the periodical texts ready to hand. I also knew the collections in which the important unpublished manuscripts resided. This was editorial work that I welcomed and felt prepared to do. I was familiar with the debates and issues that circulate through the field of scholarly editing; I understood that posthumous editors should not see themselves as assuming the identities of their authors; I knew that one should be restrained and tactful when emending the texts of a deceased author.

Editorial standards of this kind can be enunciated with great gravity in a seminar room before an audience of graduate students who won't talk back. Such standards can be set forth in a scholarly paper published in an academic journal of limited circulation. In these places it's easy to say what others should do (or should have done) with an author's literary remains or what one would do oneself if an opportunity were to present itself. In fact such principles usually *can* be put into practice in a scholarly edition if it is published by a university press. Such an edition, bearing a stiff price, will with luck and prayer sell as many as a thousand copies and might even go into a large-format paperback a few years later. But I found that these standards could not so easily be followed in the world of trade publishing for a book by Styron with a projected first printing of fifteen thousand copies, a book meant to help resurrect his name and put new work by him before his public. Nor did I possess complete authority over these texts, as I would have with novels, stories, or poems that had passed out of copyright and into the public domain. Other people with qualifications and claims as good as mine, or better, were involved. The several audiences for the texts had to be considered. The reviewers had to be kept in mind, as did potential sales figures. The aim was not to entomb Styron's writings but to *publish* them.

When Styron died in November 2006, his reputation was in limbo. He had not published a book since 1993. That volume, a slender collection of short stories called *A Tidewater Morning,* had been favorably reviewed, but no further books had been forthcoming. During the middle and late 1990s Styron had written short pieces for the *New Yorker* and the *Nation* and op-eds for the *New York Times,* but for the last six years of his life he had fallen silent. His health had not permitted him to continue writing. At his death he left behind a considerable body of literary work, both fiction and nonfiction, that had never been reprinted or collected or, in some cases, published at all. This writing came from all periods of his career—early, middle, and late. The question was how to gather and present these texts, how to add them to Styron's oeuvre so that readers and critics could arrive at an assessment of his achievement. Ideally these writings would be published in clothbound volumes by Random

House, Styron's publisher, or (for writings without much trade potential) in editions from university presses. Thus there would be a new Styron book every few years, with attendant publicity, reviews, and reassessments of his writings.

So far this has been happening. Random House published a book of Styron's personal essays in 2008 called *Havanas in Camelot;* in 2009 another collection appeared from Random House, this one of five stories based on the author's Marine Corps experiences, published under the title *The Suicide Run.* Also in 2009, Louisiana State University Press published an edition of Styron's *Letters to My Father,* a gathering of some one hundred letters written by Styron fils to Styron père between 1943 and 1953—which is to say between Styron's freshman year in college and his return to the United States after a fellowship year at the American Academy in Rome. The Library of America has agreed to publish a two-volume selected edition of Styron's writings; and a comprehensive edition of his letters is in preparation, to be edited by his widow, Rose Styron. His daughter, Alexandra, herself a novelist, has published a memoir (entitled *Reading My Father*) of the remarkable life that Styron and Rose lived at their home in Roxbury, Connecticut, and on Martha's Vineyard, Massachusetts, where they kept a summer place.

It's not unusual to see literary activity of this sort fairly soon after an author's death. F. Scott Fitzgerald, for example, died in 1940; his unfinished novel *The Last Tycoon* appeared from Scribner's in 1941, and a collection of his late nonfiction, *The Crack-Up,* was published by New Directions in 1945—both books edited by his friend Edmund Wilson. These books were followed by a collected edition of his stories, assembled by Malcolm Cowley, and by the author's "final version" of his novel *Tender Is the Night,* also edited by Cowley—both books published in 1951. All of these books presented new or uncollected work by Fitzgerald, and all brought forth discussion of central questions about his career: the relationship between his life and fiction; the tensions between art and commerce in his writings; his attitudes toward social status, money, and fame. Fitzgerald's reputation, like Styron's, was in a holding pattern during the last years of his life. His career was revived and burnished by these posthumous publications and by an excellent first biography called *The Far Side of Paradise,* published by Arthur Mizener in 1951.

This sort of activity takes place for nearly all important authors. Among the literary remains of recently deceased writers, for example, one notes an edition of an early Truman Capote novel, *Summer Crossing* (2006), never before published and thought to have been lost; a collection of Kurt Vonnegut's writings called *Armageddon in Retrospect* (2008), assembled by his son; a gathering of

Vonnegut's previously unpublished stories entitled *Look at the Birdie* (2009); an edition of John Updike's last stories called *My Father's Tears* (2009); and an edition of Gilbert Sorrentino's novel *The Abyss of Human Illusion* (2010). The process never really ends, no matter how long an author has been gone. In 2009 the scholar Laura Rattray put together a two-volume collection called *The Unpublished Writings of Edith Wharton;* in 2008 a roughed-out novel by Richard Wright called *A Father's Law* was published; in 2009 one of Hemingway's grandsons issued a new text of *A Moveable Feast,* which was itself the first Hemingway book edited and published by his widow, Mary, after his death.

The managing of Styron's literary remains fell to three people: his widow, Rose Styron, an accomplished poet and critic; Robert Loomis, his longtime editor at Random House, who had worked with many important authors; and me, his bibliographer and biographer. I collaborated with Rose and Bob on *Havanas in Camelot* and *The Suicide Run:* I gathered the texts for both books; put them into tentative arrangements, which Rose and Bob adjusted and approved; established the texts from the surviving manuscripts, typescripts, and published versions; and, with Rose and Bob, saw the books through the press and into print. At the same time I was working on *Letters to My Father*—having the letters transcribed, verifying the texts, annotating unfamiliar references from the 1940s and 1950s, arranging for illustrations, and reading proofs.

This was enormously satisfying work for me, and I am sure for Rose and Bob as well. Our intentions, so far as I can state them, were to bring William Styron's name back to the attention of readers and critics; to attract good reviews; to stimulate sales of the previous works; to sell copies of the new collections; and to make some money for the estate—which is to say, to keep the directors of Random House happy so that they will look with favor, years hence, on proposals to publish further books assembled from Styron's literary remains.

So far all has been going very well indeed. The essays in *Havanas in Camelot* were among Styron's lighter writings and showed a humorous, ironic side of his personality not in evidence in his writings on slavery, genocide, capital punishment, and clinical depression. Positive reviews of the book appeared in the *New York Times,* the *New York Times Book Review, USA Today,* the *Los Angeles Times Book Review, Newsweek,* and the *Times Literary Supplement.*[1] The *Suicide Run,* five stories taken from Styron's various efforts to write a novel about the Marine Corps, brought more good reactions. A selection from one of the narratives was excerpted before publication, in the 20 July 2009 issue of the *New Yorker,* under the title "Rat Beach." Reviews and reassessments appeared in the *Wall Street Journal,* the *Los Angeles Times,* the *New York Times Book Review,* and the *Financial Times.*[2] *Letters to My Father* was featured in the "Best New Books" section of *Reader's Digest* for September 2009 and drew a prepublication order of nine hundred copies from Barnes and Noble—unusual for a book issued by a university press.[3] *Havanas in Camelot* and *The Suicide Run* have come out in trade paperbacks; *The Suicide Run* was published as an audiobook; both volumes are now available as e-books. British editions are forthcoming. Translation rights have been sold in several countries; I learned not long ago, for example, that a translation of *Havanas in Camelot* into Chinese is to be published as an e-book.

Some of the editing that I have done to Styron's texts, however, has gone against my instincts. By this I mean relatively innocent things such as presenting pieces out of the chronological order of their composition, emending certain features silently, cutting and shaping some previously unpublished work, adding words here and there, and, in one case, composing an entire sentence. None of these offences will cause me to be sent to the penitentiary, but most of them go beyond the usual activities of a scholarly editor.

I'll be more specific about my malefactions later, but I'll pause here to say that this is precisely the sort of thing that I and others have faulted some of Fitzgerald's earlier editors for doing. Edmund Wilson, for example, made *The Last Tycoon* look much more finished than it in fact was; he switched the titles of two of the three famous Crack-Up essays when he republished them; and he changed the word "orgastic" to "orgiastic" in the last line of his edition of *The Great Gatsby.*[4] Cowley took even greater liberties, adding text to Fitzgerald's famous story "Babylon Revisited"; changing the text and chronology of "An Alcoholic Case," a late *Esquire* story; and inventing text for the author's "final version" of *Tender Is the Night.*[5]

I have therefore found myself in the odd position of undoing the work of Wilson and Cowley in the morning and, that afternoon, doing some of the same things to Styron's texts. I now understand better Wilson's and Cowley's motivations in the 1940s and 1950s. A trade book is not a scholarly edition. Trade houses do not operate as university presses do. Trade presses make decisions rapidly, move books through production quickly, and (as they should) operate for profit. They know how to identify readers and sell books. It has been an enormous advantage in resurrecting Styron's reputation to have the money and promotional muscle of Random House behind the effort. Bob Loomis, a vice president and executive editor at Random House, is the employee with the longest record of service with the firm, more than fifty years and counting. He has great influence within Random House; he knows how to tap its resources and energies. If trade houses mean to stay in business, they cannot make it a regular practice to publish editions of literary fragments, or diplomatic texts of unpublished manuscripts, or unemended versions of unfinished trial drafts. They must publish books that readers will purchase, which is also what Styron would have wanted—books that the people who followed his career would buy and read.

I have committed some sins. I have corrected factual errors, not only in essays and memoirs by Styron, which would be understandable, but also in short fiction, where a scholarly editor might leave an apparent error in the text and gloss it with a note in the back matter. I have rectified the spellings of names—of people and places and literary works; I have changed the name of a character in *The Suicide Run* from Major Wilhoite to Major Williams because, earlier in the collection, in a story written in the 1950s, Styron had created another Colonel Wilhoite. (He must have liked the name—I've found it in other drafts of unpublished writing about the Marine Corps.) I have masked, by silent emendation in the texts of letters, the fact that young William Styron was confused about *its* and *it's* until he was about twenty years old. (It was heartening to see that a writer as good as Styron once made an elementary error that I have corrected upward of twenty thousand times on student themes.) I have silently emended the string of words "a pretty girl with red hair of seventeen or eighteen" to "a pretty girl of seventeen or eighteen with red hair." I have twice changed what might be coinages by Styron to more conventional words: "incantating" has become "incantatory" and "camphorous" has been altered to "camphoraceous." I have added a sentence to a story in which a military officer rises from his desk, goes over to a window, and then, about a page later, rises from the same desk again. I added this sentence: "He returned to his desk and sat down."[6]

In *The Suicide Run,* I cut away the last several pages of a narrative entitled "My Father's House" and made it end earlier than it does in the surviving manuscript. "My Father's House" was to have been the beginning of a full-length novel. Styron wrote the first episode and then, in the extant draft, began the second episode with a loud confrontation between Paul Whitehurst, the protagonist, and an Episcopal priest whom he detests. This confrontation might have developed into something good had Styron continued with the manuscript, but he did not push the narrative forward. The text for the Random House collection had to be a self-contained story, not the beginning of an aborted novel, so I made the cuts.

In one case I refrained from emending. I let stand a factual error in one of the best items in *Havanas in Camelot,* a reminiscence of the writer Terry Southern called "Transcontinental with Tex." In this piece Styron recalled his friendship with Southern, which had its beginnings in Paris during the early 1950s. The friendship continued and eventually included a coast-to-coast airplane and railway journey that the two men made together in 1964. Styron took the trip in order to fulfill a speaking engagement at a California university; Southern was heading to Hollywood to collaborate with Christopher Isherwood on the screenplay for *The Loved One,* Evelyn Waugh's satiric novel about the American funeral industry, originally published in 1948. After a stop in Chicago to pay their respects to Nelson Algren and to see death row at the Cook County Jail, Styron and Southern ended their east-to-west odyssey on the greensward at Forest Lawn Memorial Park in Hollywood, the model for Mr. Joyboy's "Whispering Glades" in *The Loved One.* Styron recalled the scene:

> At Forest Lawn, in the blinding sunlight, our fellow tourists were out in droves. They were lined up in front of the mausoleum where the movie gods and goddesses had been laid to rest, stacked up in their crypts, Terry observed, "like pies in the Automat." Marilyn Monroe had passed into her estate of cosmic Loved One only two years before, and the queue of gawkers filing past her final abode seemed to stretch for hundreds of yards. Cameras clicked, bubble gum popped, babies shrieked. One sensed an awkward effort at reverence, but it was a strain; the spectacular graveyard was another outpost of Tinseltown.[7]

This is a memorable moment in the essay. Styron and Southern, woozy from alcoholic excess, stand in Forest Lawn and remember Monroe's allure and the fragility of her fame. But there is a problem: MM's mortal remains do not rest at Forest Lawn. She is entombed some six miles to the east, in Westwood Memorial Park in Los Angeles. Styron and Southern could not have seen tourists lining up for a look at her mausoleum in Forest Park. Styron must have invented the scene, or parts of it. This would not matter if "Transcontinental with Tex" were a work of fiction, but does matter in a nonfiction piece.

Emend or not? Changing "Forest Lawn" to "Westwood" invalidates Styron's reference to Waugh's "Whispering Glades." Removing the sentences about Monroe's crypt undercuts the entire scene. Dropping an asterisked footnote to call attention to the mistake would annoy readers and interrupt the mood that Styron is creating. In a true scholarly edition, one might include a discreet note

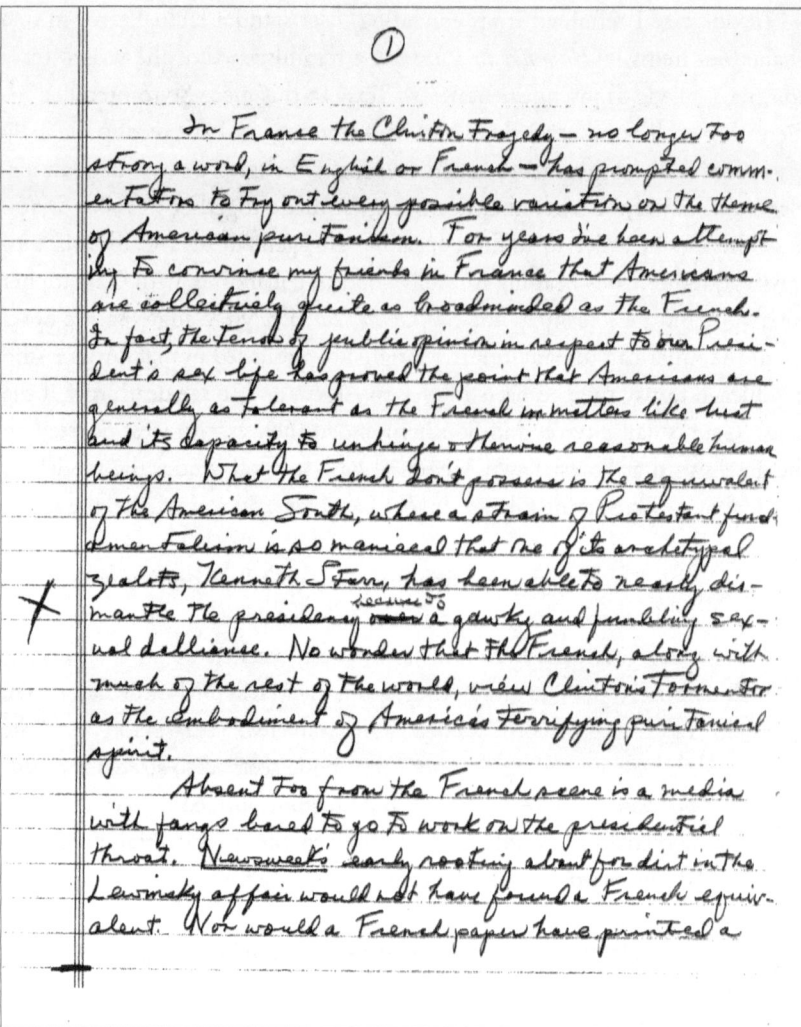

*Fig. 6* Leaf 1, holograph of Styron's statement on the Bill Clinton–Monica Lewinsky scandal. The text published in the *New Yorker* (12 October 1998) was shortened by some three hundred words to fit into the space allotted by the magazine. Irvin Department of Rare Books and Special Collections, University of South Carolina Libraries.

in the back matter, but this edition of *Havanas in Camelot* had no proper "back matter." What to do? In the end I left the text alone and did not call attention to the mistake. So far no one has said anything, at least in print. I did receive an irate e-mail from one reader, but I ignored it. I here and now shoulder my duty and reveal the error by Styron. I leave it to a scholarly editor of the future to write a gloss about this matter for the apparatus of a volume of Styron's collected nonfiction, to be published when I have myself taken my place in the great beyond.

Styron published many worthy pieces of nonfiction during his career—articles, reviews, essays, introductions, travel writings—that he did not get around to putting between hard covers. Some of his best nonfiction has never been published: a eulogy for James Dickey, a birthday tribute to the civil rights pioneer Virginia Durr, a piece on the first Iraq war that was written for *Life* magazine but canceled when the invasion by U.S. ground forces was postponed, a screed on the Bill Clinton–Monica Lewinsky scandal that the *New Yorker* cut by half. There survive among Styron's papers the false starts of at least three novels, two of them set during World War II and the other taking place in a mental ward for depressives. Eventually all of this writing, or most of it, will be put into print by Random House or by other publishers. If I were invited to do the editing, I would trim, shape, and correct the texts in the ways I did for *Havanas in Camelot* and *The Suicide Run*. The motives would be the same: to put the new writings into play in accessible texts, to attract reviews and reassessments, and to keep discussion of Styron's life and career in motion.

My work to date has had the approval of Rose Styron and Robert Loomis. All three of us missed Styron's presence and authority in assembling these books, but decisions had to be made. We tried to balance what we thought Styron would have wanted against what was feasible for Random House to publish. I believe that we proceeded as we should have, given the necessities of the task and the realities of publishing. What I should do, of course, is leave behind a record of these cuts, emendations, primpings, and polishings. I mean to do so in documents that I will put on deposit with Styron's papers at Duke University, his alma mater, but I confess that I have been tempted to conceal the evidence, keep my mouth shut, and let scholarly editors of the future, should they materialize, dig up my textual transgressions on their own. After all, that's what I've had to do with Edmund Wilson and Malcolm Cowley—uncover what they did by long hours of collating texts and noting variants.

This experience has generated in me new sympathy for keepers of the flame, among whom I must now number myself. The task of editing literary remains is not easy. Let us all reserve some sympathy for keepers of the flame.

NOTES

1. Michiko Kakutani, "Styron's Essays Give Glimpses into a Life Spent in Good Company," *New York Times*, 15 April 2008; David Leavitt, "Styron's Choices," *New York Times Book Review*, 11 May 2008; Bob Minzesheimer, "Vonnegut, Styron: Memories of Mastery," *USA Today*, 24 April 2008, 7D;

Marc Weingarten, "Havanas in Camelot," *Los Angeles Times Book Review,* 20 April 2008; Katie Baker, "A Writer's Brush with Fate," *Newsweek,* 5 May 2008; Jordan Davis, "Havanas in Camelot," *Times Literary Supplement* (London), 5 December 2008, 29.

2. Josiah Bunting III, "A Novelist's Last War Stories," *Wall Street Journal,* 3 October 2009; Nicholas Delbanco, "'The Suicide Run: Five Tales of the Marine Corps' by William Styron," *Los Angeles Times,* 1 November 2009; Elizabeth D. Samet, "Marine Dreams," *New York Times Book Review,* 11 October 2009; David Flusfeder, "The Suicide Run," *Financial Times,* 12 October 2009. See also Michael D. Langan, "Styron Echoes Fidelity to Corps," *Buffalo News,* 11 October 2009, and Kathy L. Greenberg, "Unearthed Styron Treasures Explore His Time in Marines," *Tampa Tribune,* 4 October 2009.

3. See the double reviews of *Letters to My Father* and *The Suicide Run* by Jonathan Yardley in the *Washington Post,* 4 October 2009, and by James Campbell on the front page of the *Times Literary Supplement,* 15 January 2010.

4. Wilson made the emendation in the text of *Gatsby* that was included in *The Last Tycoon, Together with The Great Gatsby and Selected Stories* (New York: Scribner's, 1941). He switched the titles of "Handle with Care" and "Pasting It Together" in *The Crack-Up* (New York: New Directions, 1945), 75, 80.

5. Barbara Sylvester, "Whose 'Babylon Revisited' Are We Teaching?" in *F. Scott Fitzgerald: New Perspectives,* ed. Jackson R. Bryer, Alan Margolies, and Ruth Prigozy (Athens: University of Georgia Press, 2000), 180–91; F. Scott Fitzgerald, "Cruxes," in Fitzgerald, *The Lost Decade: Short Stories from Esquire, 1936–1941,* ed. James L. W. West III (Cambridge: Cambridge University Press, 2008), xxiii–xxvi; Fitzgerald, *Tender Is the Night,* ed. Malcolm Cowley (New York: Scribner's, 1951).

6. William Styron, *The Suicide Run: Five Tales of the Marine Corps* (New York: Random House, 2009), 65, 132, 181, 19.

7. William Styron, "Transcontinental with Tex," *Havanas in Camelot: Personal Essays* (New York: Random House, 2008), 119.

# THE END IS NEAR

In the planning stages for a multivolume edition of an author's works, the editor typically doesn't give much thought to the eventual endgame. The final volume of the edition is many years in the future. General questions of typographical design and editorial philosophy are pleasant to contemplate early on; one can also indulge in fantasies of completeness and perfection. Matters such as attribution, inclusiveness, and editorial consistency can be dealt with in later years. But as those years pass and the final volume begins to materialize on the horizon, the editor must face facts, make decisions, and acknowledge realities.

This is the situation in which I find myself with the seventeen-volume Cambridge Fitzgerald Edition, of which I'm the general editor. Twelve volumes have been published; of the five that remain, *Tender Is the Night* is finished in manuscript, and a variorum edition of *The Great Gatsby* is nearing completion. After that will come two volumes of the late short stories—*Taps at Reveille* and *A Change of Class*. The final volume, entitled *Last Kiss*, will contain oddments and miscellaneous bits: Fitzgerald's only published play, all of his poetry, an assortment of journalism and book reviews, plus anything else I haven't been able to find a place for in one of the earlier volumes.[1] This seems a proper moment to pause and ruminate. What impelled me to undertake the editing of this collected series? To what uses will the work be put? The labor, by and large, has been enjoyable and rewarding. Does the edition really have to end?

First, some history. The project was set in motion in the 1980s by the late Matthew J. Bruccoli with the approval of the Fitzgerald Trust, which oversees Fitzgerald's literary estate, and with Cambridge University Press as the publisher. Two volumes appeared: *The Great Gatsby* in 1991 and *The Love of the Last Tycoon: A Western* in 1993. Bruccoli and the Fitzgerald Trust came to a parting of the ways a year later, largely over some emendations in *Gatsby*, and Bruccoli resigned from the project. I was asked to take over as general editor and to complete the edition. At that juncture, in 1994, I was confident that I could publish the remaining fifteen volumes in ten years, before my sixtieth birthday. I thought it would be easy. But already it's 2011, I'm sixty-four years old, and I'm now hoping to cross the finish line before I turn seventy. Most mornings I'm optimistic, certain that I'll reach the goal. But when the work drags, I feel like Cardinal Wolsey in Shakespeare's *Henry VIII:* "My highblown pride / At length broke under me," laments the prelate, "and now has left me, / Weary, and old with service" (III.ii.362–64).

One explanation for the measured progress of the Fitzgerald Edition is that I've worked on other projects—a biography of William Styron; a book about Fitzgerald and Ginevra King, his first love; and an assortment of articles and book chapters.[2] It wouldn't have been smart professionally to devote myself entirely to the Fitzgerald Edition, and, besides, editorial labor can be tedious. It's fun to poke about in a writer's life or to read love letters written by a young girl to a fledgling author. It's not much fun to run a word-by-word collation or compile a list of variants.

It's also true, however, that for the Fitzgerald Edition I've worked alone. I am the general editor of the entire series; I am also the only editor for each volume. In most multivolume editions, the general editor is the straw boss who coordinates the project and oversees the work of individual volume editors. For the Fitzgerald Edition there have been no editors for the separate volumes, only me. I made this decision when I took over the edition. I have had a series of able assistants who have performed the typical chores of textual scholarship—collating, proofing, fact-checking, and library legwork—but I have reserved all emending for myself and have written all introductions, historical glosses, and other commentary. Sharing this work with Fitzgerald scholars at other institutions should theoretically have increased the velocity of the edition, but in practice (I was convinced) the opposite would have occurred. Collaboration with others, no matter how careful their work or how serious their commitment, has in my experience always slowed a project down.

My attitude toward collaborative editing has its roots in observation of the multivolume editions undertaken in the 1960s under the aegis of the Center for Editions of American Authors, a massive editorial project sponsored by the Modern Language Association and the National Endowment for the Humanities with the intention of producing collected editions of the major nineteenth-century American authors. In the early days of the CEAA, it was a given that the best scholars and critics in a field would be invited to edit individual volumes in, say, the Emerson edition, or the Melville or the Thoreau or the Howells. The thinking was that these people could easily be trained in the basics of collating and emending. They could also write the introductions and historical notes; the general editor would assemble the results. As often as not, however, this multihanded approach did not work. Academics whose previous writings were sound and whose reputations were high did not take well to instruction in textual editing; many of them proved to be querulous and balky, unwilling to accept guidance from general editors or to have their emendations reversed. Every collaborative project proceeds at the rate of its slowest contributor. Partly as a result, many of the CEAA editions became bogged down, testing the patience of granting agencies and university presses. Many of the CEAA editions that began with great energy decades ago have still not been finished. Several of them have changed publishers; at least two seem to have come to a halt. I did not want this to happen to the Cambridge Fitzgerald Edition, so I decided to do the editing myself.

During the original planning stages for the Fitzgerald Edition, before I became involved, there must have existed a blueprint for the series, a schedule setting forth the order and content of the volumes. But if such a document was drawn up it was not passed along to me. I therefore planned out the rest of the edition on my own, deciding the contents for each of the volumes that remained, the order in which they would appear, and the editorial philosophy that would be applied to the texts. For Fitzgerald there were some obvious problems. His famous first novel, *This Side of Paradise,* published in 1920, appeared originally in an edition filled with errors: misspellings of authors' names, misused words, grammatical mistakes, and inconsistencies in chronology. Should these blunders be corrected, or should the text of the first printing be presented without emendation as a historical artifact? (I decided to correct the errors, which had embarrassed Fitzgerald and were not altogether his fault.) Fitzgerald's best-known novel, *The Great Gatsby* (1925), existed in an earlier version called *Trimalchio* that had never been published. Should it be? (Yes, of course. I published an edition in the spring of 2000.) His last completed novel, *Tender Is the Night,* went through a long, difficult gestation before its appearance in 1934; a few years after that Fitzgerald marked up a copy of the first edition in order to create an "final version," in which he rearranged the time scheme of the novel by shifting around large blocks of material. Which version of *Tender Is the Night* should be published? Should editions of both be prepared? (The Cambridge Edition will contain only the 1934 text. Fitzgerald didn't realize what a considerable can of worms he had opened by rearranging the time scheme of the novel.)

And the short stories! Fitzgerald published some 165 works of short fiction during his career, stories that vary enormously in quality, from masterpieces such as "The Diamond as Big as the Ritz" and "Babylon Revisited" to hackwork like "The Pusher-in-the-Face" and "The Ants at Princeton." The nonfiction varies similarly in quality, from superb pieces such as "The Crack-Up" and "Echoes of the Jazz Age" to negligible efforts like "The Cruise of the Rolling Junk" and "What Became of Our Flappers and Sheiks?" How and where in the edition could all of this be wedged in? Should we have done a *selected* edition? Perhaps, but everything that Fitzgerald wrote, even the most modest sketch or book review, bears traces of his genius. What should be left out, and who would decide on the exclusions? Better to include it all—assuming that the Fitzgerald Trust would allow this, of which more later.

For many of the early stories and essays, nothing survives but the published text. For the middle and late writings, however, textual evidence survives in abundance—holographs, typescripts, proofs, and relevant correspondence. The assumption had always been that Fitzgerald's stories and essays had not been meddled with by magazine editors, but I was suspicious of that notion. As it turned out I was right. Editors, especially at the *Saturday Evening Post,* made free with Fitzgerald's texts, scrubbing his stories clean of sexual innuendo and mild profanity, removing passages about drug use, expunging references to racial prejudice. Restorations have been necessary, and I have been making them.[3]

One of the major problems early on was how to arrange the short stories in the volumes of the edition. Fitzgerald published four collections of stories during his lifetime—*Flappers and Philosophers* (1920), *Tales of the Jazz Age* (1922), *All the Sad Young Men* (1926), and *Taps at Reveille* (1935). I retained the titles of these collections for individual volumes in the Cambridge series but included, in each of the volumes, not only Fitzgerald's selections for those books but also the stories that he chose *not* to reprint—the rejects from each period of his career. Thus readers would have a sense of Fitzgerald's total production. The stories that Fitzgerald chose not to reprint are not necessarily inferior goods. Sometimes he decided to exclude a story from a collection because it was too close in plot or theme to a story that he did include. (Like all authors, he repeated himself.) And sometimes he rejected a story because he had used parts of it in a novel. Those rejected stories are being preserved in the collected edition, published in the same volumes with Fitzgerald's original selections but in separate sections.

Issues of this kind must surely exist for any writer or artist whose works are being brought together in a single series. The editor's duty is to address the problems; to publish the volumes one by one; to make adjustments, often on the fly; and to cause the final volume to appear. The editor should be prepared for some disappointments at the end, however. For one thing, the edition will almost surely not be a true *omnium gatherum,* a series that includes every scrap of work, published and unpublished, that has been attributed to the author. There are always doubtful cases: it's one thing for an energetic bibliographer to place an item into a checklist on scant evidence; it's another for the editor of the collected edition to canonize that piece in a volume. This is true for Fitzgerald. Several unsigned bits of writing in the *Nassau Lit* (the Princeton student literary magazine) were attributed to him by classmates who identified them in very old age. Fitzgerald's bibliographer placed these items in the listing of the author's apprentice work, but that does not mean that they must be included in the collected edition.[4]

For Fitzgerald there are murky problems involving collaboration with Zelda Sayre, his wife. Scott and Zelda genuinely coauthored some pieces; on other occasions she wrote stories and essays that he revised but that were published under both of their names. (Magazine editors would pay more if his name was affixed.) She wrote one story, "A Millionaire's Girl," that was mistakenly published under his name alone. And the extent of work that he did on her only published novel, *Save Me the Waltz* (1932), is impossible to know from the materials that survive. A one-volume collected edition of Zelda's writings has been published, making the situation easier to manage. Inevitably, though, some items will appear both in her collected works and in his.

Finally, on the issue of completeness, there are nine stories that Fitzgerald's daughter, Scottie, decided should never be reprinted. These stories, she felt, were so far below the level of writing of which her father was capable that they should not be preserved in his collected works. Scottie died in 1986, before the Cambridge Edition was fully under way; but the Fitzgerald Trust, which assumed control of the literary rights after her death, wants to honor her wishes. Although these stories are weak, I'd like to include them in the Cambridge Edition. I have been overruled, however, and I cannot say that I'm sorry. Reading texts of these stories are easy to acquire on interlibrary loan or from the Internet.[5]

A different problem is presented by the manuscripts that Fitzgerald wrote but, for various reasons, did not publish before his death. Some of these have appeared in print over the years, including such excellent stories as "That Kind of Party" and "Dearly Beloved" and the essays "My Lost City" and "My Generation." But approximately a dozen stories that survive in manuscript have never been published. The manuscripts repose in a strongbox in a Philadelphia bank vault. These are not lost masterpieces, but they are at least as good as some of the stories that Fitzgerald *did* place and publish. Should these unpublished narratives be included in the series? The Fitzgerald Trust has decided for the present not to put them into the edition. Again I'm not terribly upset: the best of Fitzgerald's literary remains appeared long ago; nothing else that survives is of crucial importance. The next generation of Fitzgerald's heirs can decide what to do about those unpublished manuscripts.[6]

When this project is finished, it will likely be the first completed multivolume full-dress edition for a novelist of Fitzgerald's generation. An edition of Sherwood Anderson's works was launched in the 1970s but lost its momentum. No one has tackled the collected works of Edith Wharton or Sinclair Lewis. The Illinois Dreiser edition has many volumes to go, as does the Nebraska Cather edition. My friend Noel Polk has edited Faulkner's novels for the Library of America, but without full apparatus or contiguous notes. Hemingway and Wolfe are still in copyright, with no collected editions in sight. Fitzgerald is in copyright too—at least everything published after 1922 is still under copyright protection—which means that the Fitzgerald Trust makes decisions about excluding stories and leaving unpublished manuscripts in the vault. Sometimes I envy editors who are working on editions of long-dead authors for whom everything is in the public domain, but that was not the *donnée* of my edition. I'm simply grateful that the Fitzgerald Trust has allowed me to proceed with a minimum of interference—in fact, with great goodwill and cooperation.

When the final volume of the Cambridge Fitzgerald appears, the world will have a manifestly imperfect collected edition. It will be some six thousand pages long, but it will not contain all of "Fitzgerald's writings," however that term might be defined. It will be *completed* but not *complete*. The works will have been edited using various techniques, and the texts will contain some typos—three that I know of so far. I suspect that all collected editions are similarly imperfect and that editors, now and in the past, have simply sighed and acknowledged the flaws. This is a chastening experience. The consolation is that the volumes are in print and can be lined up on the shelf. Some volumes will be thick, some thin; the dust jackets and bindings might not match exactly; the front matter will vary a little from volume to volume; but the damned job will be done.

This anticipated moment brings forth long thoughts about one's original motivations for undertaking a collected edition and for staying with the work. Everyone knows the conventional aims that most scholarly editors profess. They want to purify the texts of corruption or establish standard versions of the works or preserve a series of specific texts. They want to leave a record of variants and emendations. They mean to provide readers, teachers, and critics with useful source books, volumes that include texts, accounts of composition, histories of publication, extensive annotations, and numerous illustrations—all of which can be brought into play in a classroom, a dissertation, a biography, a critical article, or a contextual study. All editors hope that their editions will have long shelf lives. Any editor's academic career will have been furthered by all of this publication, though there must be easier ways to earn a full professorship or an endowed chair. And, not least, honor will have been done to the writer.

A strong motivation for me has been the pleasure brought by intimate knowledge of Fitzgerald's writings, the daily stimulation of contemplating his words and phrases, and the frequent experience of working with his manuscripts at Princeton, where his literary papers are kept. This is absorbing work; it has put me into a kind of intimate contact with Fitzgerald that has been intensely pleasurable and quickening to the intellect. There has also been much satisfaction in assembling each volume and seeing it into print. Any volume in a full-dress edition is a piece of craftwork: it's at once an object of beauty and utility, like a complicated timepiece or a decorative box. Each volume is good to look at and hold in the hand. The parts—introduction, text, apparatus, annotations, illustrations—fit and function together to bring enlightenment. And one signs the work, just as any craftsman does. One's name is on the title page, beneath the author's name and in smaller type, but there nonetheless.

Some of my memories of this labor are good, some not so good. I recall devoting two beautiful spring days to the editing of Fitzgerald's 1936 essay "The Crack-Up." It survives in two typescripts and a magazine text. I ran the collations, contemplated the variants, and ended up making only two emendations. I added the word "only" to the Cambridge text from the second of the typescripts (the compositor for the magazine had omitted it), and I corrected the spelling of the word "Canyon." Neither emendation was of much significance; perhaps I should have spent those days outside, hiking or canoeing. But not long ago I discovered a round of textual cleansing that the *Saturday Evening Post* had performed on Fitzgerald's 1931 story "The Hotel Child," a narrative about anti-Semitism. The editors had removed all mention of alcoholism and addiction to hashish by two decadent British aristocrats who figure prominently in the story. I'll restore the passages, which explain a good deal about the behavior of those characters and, by extension, of members of their class. This was a signal discovery—and I made it while the weather outside was rotten, with the temperature below freezing and ice on the trees. I can't think of a better way in which I might have spent that time.

Must a collected edition come to an end? Can it be extended for a few more years? Can it be extended forever? Should one announce that this is an edition that will never be finished—*l'édition sans fin?* This attitude, or attitudinizing, might score points with postmodernists, but probably not with publishers, department heads, deans, the author's heirs, or one's own family members. Certainly it's tempting to prolong things for another year or two. The collected edition has given order and purpose to one's hours and days; has created a small community of graduate students and research assistants; has provided a workplace, a schedule, some grant money, and a reduced teaching load from time to time.

But from the inception of the collected edition, there will have existed an implied contract between the editor and those who are supporting the project. The understanding is that eventually the edition will be brought to a conclusion. The final volume will be placed on the shelf; the publisher will announce completion; there will be a party or a reception; the editor will become the editor emeritus. This personage, once young and vigorous, now aged and bent, will have the satisfaction of seeing the volumes lined up shoulder to shoulder. It won't be necessary for someone else to eke out the last bits of the project, after the honored editor has finally laid down the blue pencil and joined the great editorial board in the sky.

There are legitimate ways to extend the editorial labor—with paperbacks or e-books derived from the parent editions, for example, or with expanded annotations on websites that offer digital texts and pop-up variants. The discovery of new evidence is always a possibility, in which case the gray eminence can arise from the easy chair, take up the cudgels, and reenter the fray. But in most cases this won't happen. A completed edition in paper and ink, still the most durable form of publication, will have been achieved. The spines of the volumes, in matching livery, will face out in an orderly row. The edition will be done.

At the final curtain call for each of her performances, the American actress Ethel Barrymore turned to the audience and said, "That's all there is; there isn't any more." Those are sweet words to contemplate for the editor of any collected edition, especially an edition for which the end is near.

NOTES

1. Besides *The Great Gatsby* and *The Last Tycoon,* the volumes already in print are *This Side of Paradise* (1995), *Flappers and Philosophers* (2000), *Trimalchio* (2000), *Tales of the Jazz Age* (2002), *My Lost City* (2005), *All the Sad Young Men* (2006), *The Beautiful and Damned* (2008), *The Lost Decade* (2008), *The Basil, Josephine, and Gwen Stories* (2009), and *Spires and Gargoyles* (2010).

2. James L. W. West III, *William Styron: A Life* (New York: Random House, 1998); West, *The Perfect Hour: The Romance of F. Scott Fitzgerald and Ginevra King* (New York: Random House, 2005).

3. Among the stories to which restorations have been made are "Jacob's Ladder" (1927), "The Love Boat" (1927), and "Magnetism" (1927) in *All the Sad Young Men;* "A Snobbish Story" (1930) in *The Basil, Josephine, and Gwen Stories;* and "On the Trail of Pat Hobby" (1941) in *The Lost Decade.*

4. See Matthew J. Bruccoli, *F. Scott Fitzgerald: A Descriptive Bibliography,* rev. ed. (Pittsburgh: University of Pittsburgh Press, 1987), entries C19, C43, C47, C49, C63, and C64.

5. The stories are "Shaggy's Morning" (1935), "In the Darkest Hour" (1934), "The Count of Darkness" (1935), "The Passionate Eskimo" (1935), "The Kingdom in the Dark" (1935), "'Send Me In, Coach'" (1936), "The Honor of the Goon" (1937), "Strange Sanctuary" (1939), and "Gods of Darkness" (1941).

6. See Jennifer McCabe Atkinson, "Lost and Unpublished Stories by F. Scott Fitzgerald," *Fitzgerald/Hemingway Annual 1971:* 32–63.

ACKNOWLEDGMENTS

~

Of the twelve essays in this collection, ten have appeared in print, eight of them as follows:

"The Scholarly Editor as Biographer," *Studies in the Novel* 27 (Fall 1995): 295–303.
"Editorial Theory and the Act of Submission," *PBSA* 83 (1989): 169–85.
"Fair Copy, Authorial Intention, and 'Versioning,'" *Text* 6 (1994): 81–89.
"Alcohol and Drinking in *Sister Carrie*," in *Theodore Dreiser and American Culture: New Readings*, ed. Yoshinobu Hakutani (Newark: University of Delaware Press, 2000), 56–64.
"Editing Private Papers: Three Examples from Dreiser," in *Re-constructing the Book: Literary Texts in Transmission*, ed. Maureen Bell, Shirley Chew, Simon Eliot, Lynette Hunter, and James L. W. West III (Aldershot, U.K.: Ashgate, 2001), 124–36.
"Did F. Scott Fitzgerald Have the Right Publisher?" *Sewanee Review* 100 (1992): 644–56.
"The Internal Chronology of *Tender Is the Night*," *PBSA* 104 (December 2010): 527–37.
"Annotating Mr. Fitzgerald," *American Scholar* 69 (Spring 2000): 78–87.

"Double Quotes and Double Meanings in *Jennie Gerhardt*" appeared first in *Dreiser Studies* 18 (Spring 1987): 1–11. The version published here incorporates material from a followup article, "C. B. De Camp and *Jennie Gerhardt*," *Dreiser Studies* 23 (Spring 1992): 2–7. An abbreviated text of "The End Is Near" was published as "Twenty Years with Fitzgerald," *Chronicle Review*, 18 September 2009, B13–14. "Toxic Words and the Editor" and "Keeper of the Flame" are previously unpublished. The other ten essays have all been revised; several have been expanded. I am grateful to the presses and journals in which this writing first appeared for permission to reprint.

For many courtesies and much assistance over the years, I name these curators and archivists: the late Neda M. Westlake, Nancy Shawcross, Michael J.

Ryan, the late Alexander Clark, William L. Joyce, Sandra Stelts, Don C. Ske-
mer, the late Mattie Russell, John L. Sharpe III, Robert Byrd, and Patrick
Scott. At Penn State I thank Christopher Clausen and Stanley Weintraub,
both of whom are emeritus members of the faculty; Susan Welch, my dean;
and Jeanne Alexander, my longtime research assistant. My most important
debt is recorded on the dedication page.

# INDEX

*The Abyss of Human Illusion* (Sorrentino), 128
active intention, 21
Adams, Henry, 78, 89, 91, 97
*The Age of Innocence* (Wharton), 93
alcohol, in *Sister Carrie,* 39–46
Algren, Nelson, 131
*All the Sad Young Men* (Fitzgerald), 138
*An Amateur Laborer* (Dreiser), 60, 63–65
*American Diaries* (Dreiser), 60, 62–63
*American Hunger* (Wright), 35–36
*An American Laborer* (Dreiser), 71
*An American Tragedy* (Dreiser), 11
Anderson, Sherwood, 94
annotations, 115–24; editors and, 118–19; Fitzgerald
    and, 115–24; information sources for, 122
*Armageddon in Retrospect* (Vonnegut), 127
Ash, A. S., 80
Aswell, Edward C., 35

Barrie, James, 97
Barrymore, Ethel, 143
*The Basil and Josephine Stories* (Fitzgerald), 85–86
*The Beautiful and the Damned* (Fitzgerald), fair
    copy and, 32
biography, scholarly editing and, 6–7
*Black Boy/American Hunger* (Wright), 35–36
Boni and Liveright, 94
Bornstein, George, 3
Boyd, Thomas, 97
Bruccoli, Matthew J., 105, 106, 135
Bryant, William Cullen, 97

Cable, George Washington, 97
Cambridge Fitzgerald Edition, 135–43; planning
    stages for, 137–38
Campbell, Louise, 19, 20
Capote, Truman, 115, 127
Carver, Raymond, 14
*The Catcher in the Rye* (Salinger), 12, 115
Cather, Willa, 78, 140
Center for Editions of American Authors
    (CEAA), 136–37
Cerf, Bennett, 94
chariot-race sign, in *This Side of Paradise,* 116–18
Charles Scribner's Sons: business approach of,
    89–91; commercial approach for *This Side*

*of Paradise* and, 91–94; conservatism of,
    89–90; Fitzgerald and, 88–101; Princeton
    and, 96
chronology, emending, 112. *See also Tender Is The
    Night* (Fitzgerald)
collaborative editing, 136–37. *See also* Editing
Commins, Saxe, 10, 11
Cowley, Malcolm, 104, 105, 127, 129
"The Crack-Up" (essay) (Fitzgerald), 141–42
*The Crack-Up* (Fitzgerald), 127
Crane, Stephen, 11

D. Appleton, 94
*Death in the Afternoon* (Hemingway): fair copy
    of, 34; versioning approach and, 37
De Camp, Charles B., 52–55
deconstruction, 75–76
DeLillo, Don, 115
De Man, Paul, 75–76
*The Diary of H. L. Mencken,* 74; anti-Semitic
    comments in, 76–78
Dickey, James, 133
digital texts, 4–5
Djer-Kiss Girl, 120–21
documentary editing, 3–4. *See also* editing;
    versioning
Doubleday, Frank, 94–95
Doubleday, Nelson, 95
Doubleday and Co., 94–95
double quotes, in *Jennie Gerhardt,* 47–58
Dreiser, Sara (wife), 18, 23
Dreiser, Theodore, 2, 8, 11, 36, 78, 94, 140; act
    of submission and, 18–21; composition of
    *Jennie Gerhardt* by, 48–50; as diarist, 61;
    editing, 8–9; editing private papers of,
    60–72; fair copy and, 30–32, 64; nerve
    sickness of, 48. *See also* literary works of
*Dreiser Looks at Russia,* 68
*Dreiser's Russian Diary,* 60, 65–72; composition
    of, 65–68; editing challenges of, 68–71
drinking, in *Sister Carrie,* 39–46
Du Bois, W. E. B., 79
Durr, Virginia, 133

eclectic editing, 3
eclectic emendation, 3

eclectic text, 3
editing: collaborative, 136–37; nervous, 81; private papers, 60–72; scholarly, 3–8, 17–28; schools of, and delegated intention, 21. *See also* versioning
editorial courtesies, toxic language and, 80–81
editorial narratives, 2
editorial theorists, 3
editors: annotations and, 118–19; intentionalist, 2–3; interpretation and, 58; knowledge about background of, 10–11; multivolume editions and, 135–43; as narrators, 1; toxic language and, 73–86; versionist, 4
Eggert, Paul, 3
Eliot, T. S., 78
Ellis, Bret Easton, 115

fair copy, 29–30; Dreiser and, 30–32, 64; Fitzgerald and, 32–33; Hemingway and, 33–35
*A Farewell to Arms* (Hemingway), 33; versioning approach for, 37
*The Far Side of Paradise* (Mizener), 127
*A Father's Law* (Wright), 128
Faulkner, William, 10, 80–81, 140
Fay, Monsignor, 89, 95
Fecher, Charles A., 74, 80
final intention, 21
*The Financier* (Dreiser), 34; fair copy and, 31–32; versioning approach and, 37
Fisher, Dorothy Canfield, 35
Fitzgerald, F. Scott, 2, 10, 78; annotations and, 115–24; collaboration with wife Zelda, 139; Crack-Up period of, 103; fair copy and, 32–33; importance of Scribner's for, 97–98; lifetime earnings of, 94; possible publishers, 94–95; Princeton and, 96; private papers of, 61; Scribner's and, 88–101; short stories of, 138–39; toxic language and, 81–86; unpublished manuscripts of, 140; ways Scribner's made it into fiction of, 98–99. *See also literary works of*
Fitzgerald, Scottie (daughter), 139
Fitzgerald Edition, Cambridge, 135–43; planning stages for, 137–38
*Flappers and Philosophers* (Fitzgerald), 82, 138
Floradora Girls, 120–21
foul language. *See* toxic language
Frederic, Harold, 97

Gale, Zona, 97
Galsworthy, John, 97
Gates, Henry Louis, Jr., 79
Gauss, Christian, 89
Gibson, Charles Dana, 121

Gibson Girl, 120–21
*Glamorama* (Ellis), 115
glossable references, 115–24; editors and, 118–19; Fitzgerald and, 115–24; information sources for, 122
Gorky, Maxim, 97
*The Great Gatsby* (Fitzgerald), 99, 137; fair copy of, 32–33; internal chronology of, 111–12; toxic words in, 81–82; versioning approach for, 37. *See also Trimalchio* (Fitzgerald)
Greg-Bowers copy-text procedures, 3

Hancher, Michael, 21
Hastings, James, 97
*Havanas in Camelot* (Styron), 127, 128, 129, 131, 132, 133
Haydn, Hiram, 12
Hemingway, Ernest, 10, 68, 97, 128, 140; fair copy and, 33–35. *See also literary works of*
Hemingway, Mary, 128
Henry, Arthur, 18, 23, 24, 43–44, 45
Hibben, John Grier, 96
historical editing, 3–4
historical editors, 4. *See also* versioning
Hitchcock, Ripley, 11, 24, 31, 50
Huneker, James, 52

intention: kinds of, 21; schools of editing and, 21
intentionalist editing, 4
intentionalist editors, 2–3
interpretation, editors and, 58
Isherwood, Christopher, 131

James, Henry, 97
"James Watt" approach, 75
Jeffers, Robinson, 10–11, 11, 94
*Jennie Gerhardt* (Dreiser), 9, 18, 31; composition of, 48–50; De Camp's letter on, 52–54; double quotes and double meanings in, 47–58; editorial theory and, 24–27; fair copy and, 30, 32; versioning approach for, 37
Johnson, Allen, 97

Kennell, Ruth Epperson, 65–71
Kent, Frank R., 77
Klopfer, Donald, 94
Knopf, Alfred, 78
Kubitz, Estelle, 19, 20, 62
Kusell, Sallie, 19

Lanier, Sidney, 97
Lardner, Ring, 97
*The Last Tycoon* (Fitzgerald), 99–100, 127, 129

*Leaves of Grass* (Whitman), 80
Lehman, David, 76
Leslie, Shane, 88–89, 95
*The Letters of F. Scott Fitzgerald* (Fitzgerald), 61
*Letters to My Father* (Styron), 127, 128–29
Lewis, Sinclair, 140
*Lie Down in Darkness* (Styron), 12–15
Lingeman, Richard, 63
Liveright, Horace, 94
Lodge, Henry Cabot, 91, 97
*Look at the Birdie* (Vonnegut), 128
Loomis, Robert, 128, 129–30, 133

Mainwaring, Marion, 80
Marquis, Don, 97
Mencken, H. L., 36, 62, 100; anti-Semitism of, 74–78; toxic language and, 73–79
misoneism, versionist editing and, 4
Mizener, Arthur, 127
Modern Language Association, 136
*A Moveable Feast* (Hemingway), 128
multivolume editions: concluding process for, 142; editors and, 135–43; methods of extending, 142–43
*My Father's Tears* (Updike), 128
*My Life as Author and Editor* (Mencken), 80

narratives: editorial, 2; primary, 1–2; secondary, 1, 2; successful editions and, 1–2
National Endowment for the Humanities, 136
nervous editing, Fitzgerald's writings as example of, 81–82. *See also* editing
notes. *See* annotations

O'Neill, Eugene, 10, 94

Page, Thomas Nelson, 97
Perkins, Maxwell, 10, 11, 34, 89–90; *The Great Gatsby and*, 32–33
Polk, Noel, 140
Pound, Ezra, 78
*The Price Was High* (Fitzgerald), 82
primary narratives, 1–2
Princeton University: Fitzgerald and, 96; Scribner's and, 96
private papers, editing, 60–72
programmatic intention, 21

quotations, double, in *Jennie Gerhardt,* 47–58

racist language. *See* Toxic language
Rattray, Laura, 128
Rawlings, Marjorie Kinnan, 97
recapture, methods of, 2–3

Reid, Whitelaw, 97
Reynolds, Paul Revere, 35
Rider, Freemont, 52
Riggio, Thomas P., 71
*The Romantic Egotist* (Fitzgerald), 89. *See also This Side of Paradise* (Fitzgerald)
Roosevelt, Theodore, 91, 97
Roth, Philip, 115
*Russian Diary* (Dreiser), 60, 65–72

S. S. McClure, 94
Sachs, Stephen, 74
Salinger, J. D., 12, 115
Santayana, George, 97
Saroyan, William, 10
Sayre, Zelda, 139
scholarly editing, 3–4; act of submission and, 17–28; biography and, 6–7; theories of, 7–8. *See also* editing
scholarly editors: role of, 22; types of, 21
Scribner's. *See* Charles Scribner's Sons
secondary narratives, 1, 2
Sherwood, Robert, 97
Shillingsburg, Peter, 3
*Sister Carrie* (Dreiser), 9, 18, 23; alcohol and drinking in, 39–46; fair copy and, 30–31, 32; textual editing of, 45; versioning approach for, 37
Smith, Tom, 11
Sorrentino, Gilbert, 128
*The Souls of Black Folk* (Du Bois), 79
Southern, Terry, 131
Stein, Gertrude, 10
Stevenson, Robert Louis, 97
Styron, Rose, 128, 133
Styron, William, 2, 12–15; editing literary remains of, 125–33; nonfiction of, 133. *See also literary works of*
submission, act of, 17–28; Dreiser and, 18–22; scholarly editors and, 17–18
*The Suicide Run* (Styron), 127, 128, 129, 130, 133
*Summer Crossing* (Capote), 127
*The Sun Also Rises* (Hemingway), 33; versioning approach for, 37

*Tales of the Jazz Age* (Fitzgerald), 138
Tanselle, G. Thomas, 3, 21
*Taps at Reveille* (Fitzgerald), 85, 138
*Tender Is The Night* (Fitzgerald), 34, 94, 99, 106, 127, 129; fair copy of, 33; internal chronology of, 102–13; versioning approach and, 37
textual editing: of *Sister Carrie*, 45
*This Side of Paradise* (Fitzgerald), 89, 137; annotations and, 116–17; chariot-race sign in,

116–18; fair copy and, 32; publication of, 92–93; Scribner''s commercial approach for, 91–93

Tjader, Marguerite, 19

Tolstoy, Leo, 97

toxic language: editorial courtesies and, 80–81; editors and, 73–86; Fitzgerald and, 81–86; Mencken and, 73–79

*Treatise on the Gods* (Mencken), 78–79

*Trimalchio* (Fitzgerald), 32, 137; internal chronology of, 111–12. *See also The Great Gatsby* (Fitzgerald)

Turnbull, Andrew, 61

typescript books, 69

*Underworld* (DeLillo), 115

*The Unpublished Writings of Edith Wharton*, 128

Updike, John, 128

versioning: defined, 3; essence of, 35; misoneism and, 4; suitable works for, 4, 37; time required for, 3–4. *See also* editing

versionist editors, 4

Vonnegut, Kurt, 127–28

Watt, James, 75

Waugh, Evelyn, 131

Wharton, Edith, 78, 80, 81, 91, 93, 97, 140

Whitman, Walt, 80

Wilson, Edmund, 127, 129

Wolfe, Thomas, 10, 97, 140

Wright, Richard, 14, 128; versioning approach and works of, 35. *See also literary works of*

Yardley, Jonathan, 80

*Zuckerman Unbound* (Roth), 115

www.ingramcontent.com/pod-product-compliance
Lightning Source LLC
Chambersburg PA
CBHW030651110726
47901CB00002B/672